Theater of Diaspora

Parviz Sayyad

Parviz Sayyad's

THEATER of DIASPORA

Two Plays:

The Ass
and
The Rex Cinema Trial

Edited by
Hamid Dabashi

With a Foreword by
Peter Chelkowski

Mazda Publishers
Costa Mesa, California

Library of Congress Cataloging-in-Publication Data

Sayyad, Parviz
   [Khar. English]
   Theater of Diaspora: Two Plays: The Ass and the Rex Cinema Trial /Parviz Sayyad; edited by Hamid Dabashi with a foreword by Peter Chelkowski.
   p. cm.
   1. Sayyad, Parviz-- Translation into English. 2. Political plays, Persian-- Translations into English. I. Dabashi, Hamid, 1951-.
   II. Sayyad, Parviz. Muhakamah-i Sinema Reks. English. 1992.
   III. Title.
   PK6561.S4A23   1992
   891'.5523--dc20   92-37420
                                                                  CIP

Copyright © 1992 by Hamid Dabashi.
All rights reserved under International and Pan-American Copyright Conventions. No part of this publication may be used or reproduced in any manner whatsoever without written permission except in the case of brief quotations embodied in critical articles and reviews. For information address: Mazda Publishers, P.O. Box 2603, Costa Mesa, California 92626 U.S.A.

ISBN:0-939214-94-6
10 9 8 7 6 5 4 3 2 1

Mazda Publishers   1993

TABLE OF CONTENTS

ACKNOWLEDGMENTS   vii

FOREWORD   ix
    Peter Chelkowski

INTRODUCTION: PARVIZ SAYYAD AND HIS THEATER   xi
FOR THE DISPORA
    Hamid Dabashi

THE ASS   1
    Translated from the Persian with Annotations
    Hamid Dabashi

THE REX CINEMA TRIAL   83
    Translated from the Persian with Annotations
    M. R. Ghanoonparvar

ACKNOWLEDGMENTS

This book has been in preparation for a number of years. It began with my translating Parviz Sayyad's play *The Ass*. It continued with my asking Peter Chelkowski to write a foreword to it. Then I asked M. R. Ghanoonparvar to translate *The Rex Cinema Trial*. In the meantime I pestered Parviz Sayyad with inquiries to write an introduction to the volume. He reluctantly submitted. My interest in these two plays and in Parviz Sayyad himself stems from my concerns with various aspects of the post-Revolutionary *angst* that has forcefully held Iranians, in or out of their homeland, in its powerful grip. Parviz Sayyad's theater of diaspora captures a particularly troubling phase in this post-Revolutionary anxiety. I wish to pause and dwell in this anxiety for its obvious historical and theoretical implications for that generic totality we easily identify (and dismiss) as a "revolution." The artistic, dramatic, and literary aspects of these plays are to be judged and evaluated on an entirely different set of criteria than a sociological perspective on their historical significance. That historical significance is also above and beyond the politics of these plays, their revolutionary or anti-revolutionary preoccupations. It is the concern with the condition of a post-revolutionary exile, and the theater it produces, not the politics and aesthetics of Sayyad himself, that has led me and those who have joined me in this project to translate and reflect on these plays.

When I started translating *The Ass*, I did not anticipate the number of debts that I would have to incur before it was completed. I would like to thank a number of individuals who were instrumental in seeing this translation through its various stages. First and foremost, I am grateful to my wife, Afsaneh A. Dabashi, not only for typing the several drafts of the play but also for her invaluable assistance in helping my translation read more accurately the nuances of the original. Parviz Sayyad himself was very generous, once he overcame his initial reluctance, with me in answering my questions—sometimes so profuse that bordered with inquisition. Peter Chelkowski read my translation of *The Ass* with care and gave me valuable advice and encouragement. The occasion of his teaching at the University of Pennsylvania during the summer of 1986 gave me the opportunity to ask him for a foreword to this translation. He graciously accepted and indebted me and the readers of this translation with the insights of the leading scholar of the Iranian performing arts. Thea Diamond, of the English Department at the University of Pennsylvania, and Benjamin Weaver, of the Department of English and Comparative Literature at Columbia University, read an earlier draft of my translation of *The Ass* and helped me make certain sentences behave themselves. As a playwright, Thea Diamond also brought a sharp eye and a sensitive ear to the staging aspects of the play that I would have otherwise missed. M. R. Ghanoonparvar responded favorably and quickly to my request to translate *The Rex Cinema Trial*. He also accepted the arduous task of reviewing both our translations repeatedly. I do not know of any translator more competent than he to have asked to join me in making these plays available in English. I am grateful for his contribution and honored by his friendship. Finally, I thank Selma Pastor for preparing the final manuscript in her usual expert manner.

Hamid Dabashi

FOREWORD

In a chapter entitled "Popular Entertainment, Media and Social Change in Twentieth Century Iran," which I wrote several years ago for the *Cambridge History of Iran*, vol. VII, I devoted three pages of the ninety-six-page manuscript to Parviz Sayyad, subtitling the piece "Parviz Sayyad—the Bridge between the Past and the Present."

Parviz Sayyad made his entrance onto the Iranian stage and into Iran's film and television arena at a time when much of traditional Iranian entertainment and performing arts had ceased to exist, or had undergone drastic transformation, moving from their natural urban environment into the rural areas. In some cases, particular forms had even died out completely. This state of affairs resulted from Iran's rapid urbanization, accompanied by the fast growth of new means of communication and major shifts in the socioeconomic and political structure of the country.

Prior to that time, entertainment in Iran, and for that matter in other countries of the Middle East, was connected to seasonal festivals, religious holidays, weddings, birthdays, circumcisions, etc. However, when Sayyad began his career in the entertainment world, it had become a leisurely pastime, in no way influenced or effected by the calendar. This change was due mainly to the spread of new and popular forms of entertainment such as film, television, radio, the cabaret stage, and Western theater. It can be said that the modern media created major change in the whole life pattern of Iranian society. The rapid Westernization of the country has almost eliminated the traditional performance forms such as *ruhowzi*, the Iranian improvisatory comedic theater; *naqqali*, story telling; and *ta'ziyeh*, the passion play.

Parviz Sayyad very nearly rescued these traditional Iranian forms of performance single-handedly from oblivion. These traditional entertainment modes make up Sayyad's personality. His paternal and maternal ancestors had been engaged in the performing arts for many years. He was born, in fact, "en route" when a performing troupe which his father belonged to was moving from one locale to another in the Caspian Sea province of Gilan. Sayyad grew up with the troupe and began performing himself as soon as he could walk.

In high school, Sayyad began to exercise his skill and talent as a playwright, although his presence on a national scale did not become apparent until the mid-1960s when he actively championed the traditional arts of performance. His role in this endeavor is similar to that of Carlo Gozzi's in Italy at the end of the Eighteenth Century, when Gozzi tried to prolong the life of the Commedia dell'Arte as a meaningful cultural institution for the people. Like the Commedia dell 'Arte, the Iranian *ruhowzi, naqqali,* and passion play possess a store of symbolism and history which help the audience cope with the realities of their difficult present, permitting them to project themselves into the romanticized past and strengthening their hopes for the future.

While it is true that Sayyad is versatile in all indigenous forms of Iranian entertainment, and that he made a point of demonstrating them to various audiences, his main achievement has been in projecting the indigenous forms onto the imported ones and amalgamating them, be it in his many television serials, in feature films, or in theatrical productions.

The cross-breeding of tradition and modernity brought about by Sayyad is visible in the growth of the dramatis personae, plot development, and especially in staging techniques. The humor and laughter in many of Sayyad's productions are taken almost directly from *ruhowzi*, softening the rigid codes and mores of the society, and is used as an outlet for grievances against harsh autocratic governments, rulers, and fathers. Sayyad brought the cathartic qualities of the *ta'ziyeh* into many of his films and theatrical plays. In the theatrical productions Sayyad uses the *ta'ziyeh* technique of breaking down barriers between the actors and the audience; his theater is a "total theater," uniting viewer and performer as one. Sayyad possesses what great men of contemporary Western theater like Jerzy Grotowski and Peter Brook are looking for; the heroes of Sayyad's work often have the qualities of the great classical heroes of Persian literature who came down to the present via the one-man show of *naqqali*.

At the same time that Sayyad is a traditionalist, he is a modern director, actor, playwright, and visionary, almost bordering on avant-garde theater and film. The manuscript for the *Cambridge History of Iran*, in which I dubbed Sayyad the "Bridge between the Past and the Present," was written before Sayyad's artistic creativity started to have an impact on a new audience—the Iranians now living in exile. Through his films and theatrical productions, Sayyad now becomes a "bridge" between Iran proper and diaspora. He becomes a vital link between the immigrants and the soil of Iran. And, though that connection helps many in the audience to recharge their patriotic batteries, for others it is like the Zoroastrian bridge of consciousness of good and evil which hangs between heaven and the place of damnation.

Peter Chelkowski
New York University

INTRODUCTION

PARVIZ SAYYAD AND HIS THEATER FOR THE DIASPORA

You are welcome, masters. Welcome all. I am glad to
see you well. . . . O,
Old friend, why, thy face is valanced since I saw thee
last. . . .
—*Hamlet*, Act II, Scene II

Long before the theater of the Iranian diaspora, or its art and literature, its active and agitated imagination, can find its own language and tone, there are mighty forces of disenchantment and soul-searching that will have to be charted and exhausted. Before all the post-revolutionary anxieties of the disillusioned diaspora are artistically charted, before all the goblins damned of "who lost the Revolution" are exorcised, it may very well be that this generation of the Iranian artists abroad has led to the next. But in the interim, the old and familiar faces, valanced since we saw them first and last, will have to assume the posture of new and moving traces of a life in exile. Having produced and performed for the pre-Revolutionary Iranians in his homeland, Parviz Sayyad is now acting out the (in)articulate despairs and confusions of the diaspora. His story and those of a battery of characters he has created are geared in a metamorphosis not quite unlike the central event of *The Ass*, troubled by a range of post-Revolutionary soul-searching and (false) accusations not very dissimilar to those of certain characters in *The Rex Cinema Trial*.

For generations to come, Iranians, particularly those in exile, have a lot of self-criticizing to do. The two plays translated here are prime examples of this enduring urge. It is one of the conditions of exile that it affords reflections on the nature of time past, mistakes made, opportunities lost, anxieties postponed. Those who stay there and pay for their momentary enthusiasm with their misdirected anger experience a kind of collective absolution, a final coming to terms with reality, an atonement once and for all. For those who leave there is a lingering undercurrent of accountability, an irresistible urge to pose "But why," a relentless insistence to ponder "But you see. . . ."

My choice of having these two plays translated stems from a continuous concern with the record of the Iranian diaspora as it comes to terms with its exilic realities, its revolution betrayed, misdirected, wronged. This is an aspect of the Iranian Revolution of 1979 that no student of it can afford to ignore. In the vast expanse of the American migration (add European, Asian, Australian, etc.), Iranians are coming to terms with their share or denial of what happened in, some say to, their homeland more than a decade ago. No generation of the Iranian diaspora will ever get over the cataclysmic events of 1979. In its enduring memory, the Islamic Revolution of 1979 matches the Arab invasion of the Seventh Century for the continued efforts of the Iranian exile in some form of self-definition or another.

A popular entertainer of considerable appeal, Parviz Sayyad is one of the leading chronographers of the Iranian diaspora in its age of exilic pause—before it decides to go one way or another, or perhaps nowhere at all, permanently on the periphery. That when he talks Iranians listen has a history.

PARVIZ SAYYAD: ARTIST/ENTREPRENEUR

"There is nothing more difficult for me than to tell you about my own work." Despite this initial dismissive answer Parviz Sayyad conceded to my inquiries, probing, as I did, into his work in modern Iranian theater and cinema. Modesty, whether true or false, has been the chief negational force that has occasioned the Iranian artist to attend history incognito. Of course, I knew Sayyad. Perhaps more than he thought I did. But the public mythologies that usually accompanied an artist in the old regime were particularly acute about Sayyad, and this made an unmitigated look at his artistic career all the more necessary. Those mythologies have not altogether disappeared among the newly formed Iranian diaspora. They have merely changed form or, occasionally, content. The diaspora has its own logic, or excuse, for creating myth; however, that logic may be different from the one operative in the homeland. The elements of the differentiae, one set metamorphosed into another, is as much relevant in the social psychology of the diaspora as it is in its theater. The mythology is at once political and artistic, and it is applied to politicians and artists interchangeably. Because of the nature of his art, Sayyad has been particularly receptive to such public myths. Staying clear of such fictitious forces that surround a public figure can be attempted. The degree of success is a different story.

Parviz Sayyad is one of the most prolific artists in modern Iranian theater, television, and cinema. Both before and after the Islamic Revolution he has been relentlessly at work. Perhaps the most unique aspect of Sayyad's work is that he successfully manages to strike a balance between producing popular entertainment, without bordering on vulgarity, and then in turn financing such highly acclaimed artistic masterpieces as *Tabi'at-e bi-jan* (The Still Life, 1974). In his popular movies and television series he brought social sensitivity to an otherwise degenerating industry. By accepting the financial risk of critically acclaimed but unpopular movies, he helped to provide the young Iranian cinema with the opportunity to give the world a superb director like Sohrab Shahid-Sales, perhaps the finest lyrical poet in modern Iranian cinema. In the midst of a highly bifurcated artistic tradition, Sayyad bridged a gap (quite different from that articulated by Peter Chelkowski in his Foreword) that so deeply separated the increasingly elevated preoccupations of an intellectual elite, from one side, and the relentlessly degenerative public entertainments, from the other. Given the political exigencies that accompanied this otherwise normal division of taste and spirit, Sayyad's self-imposed task was not an easy one. He did not always succeed. A considerable degree of political engagement accompanied the artistic and literary tastes of the divided audience. Sayyad's success or failure in uniting this division will have to be considered in the context of his biography.

Parviz Sayyad was born on January 20, 1937, in the city of Lahijan, some fourteen miles from the Caspian shore. He lost his mother, Mahjabin, when he was two years old. His father, ʿIsa, married several times after Parviz's mother died. One of his stepmothers was chiefly responsible for Parviz's upbringing. Parviz left his parents quite early in his life, and not sooner than when he was fourteen years old he was living independently. Throughout his early education he had to support himself by working half-time during the school year and full-time in summer.

His father was a poet and an actor. He played in the traditional Iranian passion play, *taʿziyeh*. He began by playing the role of ʿAli Akbar, Hoseyn's son, and continued until he was old enough to play ʿAbbas, Hoseyn's half-brother. He was also a *naqqal*, the traditional performer who recites stories from the *Shahnameh* and other Iranian folk tales and mythologies. ʿIsa Sayyad was one of those rare individuals who still presented the oral tradition of *Shahnameh-khani* (recitation of the *Shahnameh*). In the direct line of the oral tradition, ʿIsa Sayyad had composed long poetic narratives about mythical heroes and episodes of the *Shahnameh*. These narrative poetries would fully develop a particular figure from the ancient Iranian folk tales.

Sayyad never developed a close relationship with his father. Yet occasionally he asked him to participate in theatrical or television productions of works with specific folkloric themes. There are probably tapes of his performances still preserved in Iran. ʿIsa Sayyad died in Tehran in 1975. He was survived by Parviz and his younger brother, Homayun.

Parviz Sayyad began his early education in Tehran. He received his high school diploma in 1957, majoring in literature. After two years of mandatory military service he entered the University of Tehran, first in law school and then in the department of economics. He graduated in 1968 with a B.A. in Economics. Immediately after the Revolution he came to the United States in 1980 and entered the City University of New York, with the intention of earning his Ph.D. in theater. He was a Ph.D. candidate before he left CUNY. His dissertation, still to be completed, was on the traditional Iranian passion play, *taʿziyeh*.

Sayyad's artistic activities began by playwriting when he was still in high school. He also published his poems and short stories in such literary journals as *Ketab-e Hafteh* and *Ferdowsi*. One of his early plays won a national prize, awarded by *Namayesh*, a leading journal of the performing arts. Since the award was co-sponsored by the Office of the Performing Arts (*Edareh-ye Honarha-ye Deramatic*), a government agency established to promote and facilitate theater, Parviz Sayyad became immediately recognized by some of the leading figures in the Iranian theater, e.g., ʿAli Nasirian, ʿEzatollah Entezami, and ʿAbbas Javanmard. Sayyad was still in high school when his plays, such as *Mosta'jer* (The Tenant, 1965), were being staged by such leading directors as Davoud Rashidi.

Sayyad himself narrates the story of how, while he was still eighteen years old, he found his way into television:

> I went to collect my prize, which I had won in a playwriting competition, from the Office of the Fine Arts. They said I had to see a certain Dr. Forugh who was then the Director of this Office. Dr. Forugh could not believe that an eighteen year old chap could be the winner of that competition. I asked him if he would submit my play to the actors in his office to be recorded for television. At the time they had a theater program on television once a week for an hour. I told him that instead of performing the translated foreign plays, his actors could stage my play. He said they only had one hour a week and for that they needed short plays. I told him I will write short plays for you; and I did. This was the beginning of Iranian one-act plays. The first play I wrote for them was called *Talisman*. This was immediately staged by their best artists, Nasirian and Entezami.

The theme of *Talisman*, verifying Peter Chelkowski's remarks, was a modern adaptation of Rostam and Sohrab. A retired warrant officer of gendarmie volunteers to arrest a certain rebel who had killed a number of gendarmes. His fellow officer, who has joined him merely in hopes of collecting the prize put on the rebel's head, discovers that financial gain is not the motive of his fellow retired officer. He has come out of retirement on the pretext of finding the rebel, just to be once again in the territory where many years ago he had won the favors of a beautiful gypsy woman. After their brief encounter, the officer had never seen the woman again. She, as he finds out, had to escape her tribe in order to save herself and her illegitimate son. The retired officer finally tracks the rebel down to a teahouse and is forced to kill him in self-defense—only to find out that he is his own son.

After *Talisman*, Sayyad wrote three other short plays, which were also staged by Nasirian and Entezami: *Dead End*, *The Point of No Return*, and a poetic narrative called *The Sad King*.

> These established my reputation as a playwright . . . and when the invitation from the Institute of International Education was received by the Ministry of Art and Culture

INTRODUCTION   xv

to send two young artists to the United States, I was the first choice, despite the fact that I was not a member of the inner clique.

In 1963, Parviz Sayyad's success resulted in a fellowship by the Institute of International Education, through which he was able to come to the United States to observe and study theater. Following this trip, Sayyad decided to concentrate on drama, leaving aside both poetry and short stories.

The bureaucratic difficulties in working through governmental agencies forced Sayyad to establish an independent center for performing arts. The Independent Group for Performing Arts (*Goruh-e Azad-e Namayesh*) was established in 1966. From this year forward, Sayyad made that group the leading center for performing arts. Mainly through this center, Sayyad produced more than forty short plays for television, and five long pieces for stage. Three of these five longer plays have been published: *Mosta'jer* (The Tenant, 1965), *Mardi keh Mordeh Bud va Khod Nemidanest* (The Man Who Had Died and He Did Not Know It Himself, 1969; but not released because of censorship until one year before the Revolution), and more recently *Khar* (The Ass, 1983). A consummate performer, Sayyad has always been more interested in the live stage than in the printed page: "I have never been too keen about publishing my plays. In fact, I have always written my plays after I had already committed them to stage."

As Peter Chelkowski points out in his Foreword, Sayyad has also been active in rejuvenating the traditional modes of the performing arts in Iran. He has collected, organized, and staged many pieces in the *ta'ziyeh*, *naqqali*, and *ruhowzi* traditions. Sayyad's resuscitation of the artistic traditions native to the Iranian culture not only gave them a fresh medium of expression, but provided them with an opportunity to influence the modern theater more directly.

Perhaps Sayyad's most enduring contribution to the Iranian theater has been his adaptation of modern techniques in creating modes of performing arts indigenous to Iran and with specifically Iranian themes and motifs. At a Shiraz Art Festival, Sayyad staged the theatrical version of a narrative poem by Manouchehr Yekta'i, *Falgush* (a traditional mode of fortune telling by sitting on a street corner and interpreting the words overheard from the conversations of passersby). Using *naqqali* and *ta'ziyeh* techniques Sayyad produced a theatrical version of this poem and called it *Experimenting with the Performing Possibilities of a Poem*. Peter Brook saw this play in a teahouse in Shiraz. This, incidentally, was the beginning of a much celebrated idea of staging plays in non-theatrical atmospheres. Peter Brook considered this play as something quite innovative and asked Sayyad to stage it in a theater festival in Nancy. But Sayyad recalls that he was not able to attend this festival "because of the 'particular attention' that the government paid to independent institutions."

Sayyad began his movie career in 1969 by playing the role of *Hasan Kachal* (Hasan the Bald) in a cinematic rendition of a traditional folk hero. In 1970 he directed *Samad va Qalicheh-ye Hazrat-e Soleyman* ("Samad and Solomon's Carpet"), for which he wrote the screenplay and acted the leading role of Samad. Altogether Sayyad has been involved in the production of twenty-four movies, as actor, script writer, director, or producer, or all at once. In twelve of these movies he has been both script writer and director. He was the producer of one of the most critically acclaimed movies in the history of Iranian cinema, *Tabiʿat-e bijan* (The Still Life, 1974). Sayyad also wrote the screenplay and directed *Dar Emtedad-e Shab* ("Along the Night," 1976), one of the most successful Iranian movies.

Sayyad has an equally impressive record on television. He wrote the script for, produced, directed, and acted in more than four hundred episodes of various shows whose reputations became synonymous with his.

Sayyad's artistic achievements have not gone totally unnoticed. He has been a recognized name in many international festivals. He participated in the Shiraz Arts Festival (*Jashn-e Honar-e Shiraz*) three times, introducing the traditional Iranian theater, both *taʿziyeh* and folk plays, to an international audience. In the Berlin Film Festival in 1974, his production of *The Still Life* won four awards, including the International Critic Award for best picture. His other movies have also been recognized in Moscow, London, and Paris film festivals.

It is impossible to do justice, in the course of a short introduction, to the range of complex characters that Parviz Sayyad has created, portrayed, and made massively popular. These characters, e.g., Samad and Hasan Beljiki, became not only household names but common symbolic references in a spectrum of political and cultural contexts.

Perhaps the greatest artistic creation of Parviz Sayyad in terms of its cultural implications has been Samad. This endearing character was developed from an inconspicuous beginning in a television show where a rustic boy, Samad Aqa, was innocently suspected of an unidentified murder. Although in this episode the greenhorn boy was nameless, he immediately became so popular that Sayyad created a whole storyline around him, and as a result perhaps the most successful Iranian television series, *Adventures of Our Man, Samad*, was launched.

Samad's character was right from the deep Iranian village life: shrewd yet innocent, canny yet innocuous, crafty yet innoxious, quick-witted yet far from malicious. He questioned every authority yet led a decent life. His fear of the only figure of authority he respected, his mother, *Naneh-Agha*, was the supreme inner inhibition that sustained his civility. His love for Leyla was pure, sublime, almost Platonic, but far from sentimental. With his cohorts, ʿEynollah, Kadkhoda, Sarkar Ostovar, etc., he was the chief protagonist. His simplicity would outwit the canniest of them all. His sole weapon was his

INTRODUCTION   xvii

pointing finger, which he always threatened to use but rarely did. Every gesture of Samad was at once innocent and shrewd. He would thus create hilarious scenes that border on bitter irony. In an episode Samad and his companions were imprisoned in the village police station. He easily managed to escape his cell just to come up to the roof and shout at a gendarme who was in his way to buy *chelow-kabab*: "Don't you forget to get me some tomatoes too!" Then he returns to his cell.

Samad and his gang became so popular that their names and experiences were household anecdotes. Even in the political scene more than once the prime minister, the late Amir ʿAbbas Hoveyda, or other politicians, would resort to a line of Samad to drive a point home. According to a commonly believed report, the accuracy of which is here irrelevant, the late prime minister Hoveyda never attended cabinet meetings on Wednesday nights, when Samad was aired.

Between 1970 and 1978, Sayyad made nine Samad movies. Many of these movies and three hours of the thirteen-hour television series never made it through the government censorship. His last Samad movie, *Samad Gur Beh Gur Mishavad* ("Samad out of the Frying Pan and into the Fire") was destroyed, according to Sayyad, by the officials of the Islamic Republic.

But Samad was resurrected in the United States. Sayyad staged *Samad Goes to War* first in 1984 for the Iranian community in Los Angeles and subsequently in other major U.S. cities. The resurrection of Samad was welcomed heartily by the Iranian diaspora; tens of thousands reminisced with this homely character in San Diego, San Jose, San Rafael, Sacramento, Portland, Seattle, Minneapolis, Chicago, Detroit, Philadelphia, Boston, New York, Washington, Atlanta, Miami, Houston, Dallas, and Phoenix. "Baptized" in Los Angeles, Samad, as the prototypical of the Iranian diaspora, became Americanized. Sayyad later directed a sequel to *Samad Goes to War*. *Samad Returns from War* traced the adventures of the endearing boy as he and his friends return from the battlefields of the Iran-Iraq War to face their devastated village, remember their abandoned dreams. Following their American debut, the two Samads, to and from war, were taken to a European tour in the summer of 1990.

Samad was probably matched, in his popularity, by another character that Sayyad created and acted in another television series, *Okhtapus* ("Octopus"). Hasan Beljiki (Hasan from Belgium), the chief figure of this series, was a charlatan *par excellence*. A quacksalver of ingenious verbosity, Hasan Beljiki constantly talked but never said anything. He was always neatly dressed, soft-spoken, persuasive, argumentative, and charming. He would ultimately win the discussion, but by then he had also trivialized the point to nullity. The characters who appeared with him, e.g., Aqa-ye Qatebeh (Mr. The Majority of the People), Hazrat-e Ostad (His Excellency the Professor), Roqiyeh (Samanta), an upwardly mobile maid with a confused morality but high aspirations, and Manizheh, the secretary of the group and the interlocutor between the cast and the audience, captured some prominent character types from the heart of the pre-Revolutionary Iranian society. Through one hundred and fifty episodes, Sayyad produced the most comprehensive gallery of Iranian popular culture traits in *Okhtapous*. With a remarkable combination of anti-heroes, set in non-plots, Sayyad produced hour-long episodes of utter non-events. The symbolically loaded language of *Okhtapous*, constantly shifting from a pun on words to a similitude of actions, was achieved with such subtlety that it not only eluded the censor officials but also the casual observer.

THE ASS

The Ass is the first theatrical production of Sayyad after the Islamic Revolution. After this play he also staged *Samad Goes to War* and *Samad Returns from War*. Other than these three plays, Sayyad has also produced and directed two feature films, *Mission* and *Checkpoint*. Both *Mission* and *Checkpoint* are also deeply involved examinations of the Iranian diaspora in its moments of crisis, its precise instance of trying to find out what it is that it is doing in "Emrika [America]." The story of *Checkpoint* evolves around an actual event during the Hostage Crisis when President Carter, as a measure against the Islamic Republic, invalidated the visas of Iranian students in the United States. The central tension of the movie is around six Iranian students who in returning back with their friends from Canada are denied entrance into the United States. As in *Checkpoint*, Sayyad's *Mission* transplants many inherently Iranian problems from their natural context into an alien atmosphere. An assassin who has been sent to kill a former member of SAVAK, the Iranian secret police, in the United States is led to discover certain ambiguities and doubts in his former convictions and certainties.

The stage production of *The Ass* outside Iran is not just a matter of political necessity. The audience of *The Ass* is decidedly the Iranian diaspora. Although the entire episode of this play, unlike the movie *Mission*, happens in Iran sometime after the Islamic Revolution, the language of its delivery is addressed primarily to the diaspora. There is a peculiar metamorphosis here, amplifying the thematic metamorphosis of man/ass in the play. The two metamorphoses complement each other. Whereas the thematic metamorphosis is biological/mental, the other metamorphosis, that of the audience, is spatial/temporal. The story happens in Iran, but it is staged in the United States; the diaspora audience sees the play in the United States, but is transferred to Iran. The plot of the play is very simple. Days after the success of the Islamic Revolution, a woman wakes up in the morning and sees her husband turned into an ass from the neck up. As the Iranian diaspora watches the woman confronting the problem, in effect accusing all who participated in the revolution of stupidity, the two metamorphoses compound. The self-reflective accusation of stupidity is underlined by a poem of the Iranian mystic poet Jalal al-Din Rumi (1207-1273) that appeared on the announcement sheet of the stage production of the play:

> O Friends listen to this story!
> In truth it is our own history.

As it moves, *The Ass* is a soul-searching, self-incriminating indictment. It reenacts the revolutionary experience as it first revived and then tormented an excited and mobilized nation. The characters of the play, the Husband, the Wife, the Brother, the Father, the Lawyer, the Physician, and the Writer, all have had a stake, one way or another, in the Revolution. The woman's encounter with her male counterparts primarily gives them the opportunity to reveal their experience or notion of the Revolution. In the diaspora audience, too, everybody is a husband, a brother, a father, a physician, a lawyer, or a writer. The actors act out the audience.

The theater of the Iranian diaspora, now just beginning to take shape but undoubtedly to flourish further, will continue to have the self-flagellation theme as one of its main leitmotifs. Precisely at those moments where comedy subtly metamorphoses into tragedy, the staging of *The Ass* becomes an occasion of collective self-flagellation, a commiserating in exile, a communal atonement with a relentless sense of loss, a remembrance of things past with the full power of nostalgic illusion. Commiseration, as all acts of redemptive suffering, is at once cleansing and distortive. Having laughed at their collective miseries, the Iranian diaspora leaves the public staging of *The Ass* to their private puzzlement of what exactly are they doing in "Emrika." The laughter conceals and thus aggravates the bewilderment. But the humorous self-flagellation has also intensified the conviction that *az mast keh bar mast* ("we suffer the consequences of our own deeds").

But if the blame is universal to all husbands, brothers, fathers, writers (lovers), physicians, and lawyers, then who is the heroine: the symbol of righteousness, the counterbalance of all such male wickedness that has been the terror of the earth? This leads to the Wife, the character who embodies the central tension of the play. Her main disposition towards the metamorphosed Husband is centered around the accusation that "He's not opposed to anyone or anything." This disappointment motivates the entire play. But to begin with the most obvious, the whole question of metamorphosis is not all that straightforward. The Wife's attempt to mobilize her dead figures of authority in order to settle the emerging *modus vivendi* has tipped the balance towards her only because the Husband tricks the audience, as well as the Wife, in misrepresenting his true identity. In the last scene when he takes off the mask all that remains from his asshood is precisely that:

a mask. Hold this trick a constant and there is no reason to believe that the Wife is actually right in insisting that her husband has turned into an ass. But if this uncertainty is carried forward, as opposed to the illusory evidence to the contrary, then the entire self-righteous episodes of her raising the "j'accuse" finger is rather an ill-fated enterprise. The foundation of her arguments, and the audience's sympathy with her, is based on an illusion, deliberately crafted by the Husband.

The illusion is amplified elsewhere in the play. The Wife, with the tacit approval of the Husband, boasts of how "different" (read liberal and liberated) they used to be. But on the stage, while she is reminding him (and herself) how "different" he has been from other (traditional) husbands, she is cleaning the table, going back and forth to the kitchen, talking to the Husband who is sitting comfortably, reading his morning paper, without lifting a finger to help. Now, this trivial incidence, and precisely in its triviality, is a rather "reactionary" background to an otherwise liberal dialogue.

Such discrepancies of dialogues and actions, betraying a deeper dichotomy of professed norm and blatant behavior, is amplified further in the play. The Wife's initial reluctance to discuss their problem with an outsider, "even a doctor," is subsequently trivialized when she, except for fear of embarrassment (and not loyalty to her husband), wants to call all the neighbors in to watch her husband, or when she invites an array of experts/witnesses to pass judgment on this man-turned-ass. She says one thing, and quite loudly, but does another, quite self-righteously. The discrepancy is not just a matter of her confusing ideological labels for political realities; it also reflects a comfortable and selective configuration of such problematic realities that would fit and support her slogans.

Through this strategy she is quite successful in convincing the Husband that he, and consequently all other male characters, have turned indeed into asses. The final and deceptively obvious victory of the Husband to turn her into an ass is just a parody—yet another self-righteous condescension of the Wife. It cannot be more than a mere condescension simply because the Husband has just finished comparing her with Hafez, Nima, and God Himself (all males, despite the obvious hierarchy). The woman-turned-God (she is an atheist anyway) is the logical counterbalance of the man-turned-ass. As false metamorphosis, the two ends of this spectrum reveal the inner anxieties of a turbulent culture in exile. The fact that the woman has the sympathy of the audience (the Husband is actually seen with an ass's head) is itself an indication of the self-flagellating diaspora.

Her professed anarchism has a feminist twist. She admits she has "nothing to rely on in this world other than love." Having nothing to rely on promotes quite a recalcitrant predisposition; it renders the baseless anarchist imbued with a persistently transgressive mentality. But initiating every act *ex nihilio*, because of having "nothing to rely on," is bound to be self-contradictory. The

INTRODUCTION   xxi

Wife is at once denying her enduring political culture by rebelling against it, and yet affirming it by yielding, however unwittingly, to its semantics of authority. Her notions of "The West," to the degree that they reveal her cultural relocation, stop at an artificial, conspicuously shallow, level of exposure to certain evidently voguish and radically contemporaneous episodes. As the geranium she so dearly loves, under the concealing rubric of its reminding her of her mother, the woman has no roots and grows on just about any air.

The woman's understanding of "love" exposes her inner contradictions even further. She has nothing to rely on other than love, yet she exposes her husband, whom she professes to love, to ridicule and humiliation by mobilizing every figure of authority she knows: her Brother who despises the Husband, the Father who is not particularly fond of him either, the Lawyer and the Writer who dislike him because of his winning the love of a woman they had once fancied, and the Physician with an authoritative stamp of his approval. The fact that to her eyes—and ours—all her figures of authority will turn into asses, after she has virtually made asses out of them anyway, diminishes nothing of her original scheme to prove to the Husband that he is physically transfigured into an ass. This scheme will make of a remotely romantic moment of her encounter with her former lover, when she inquires about the state of her beauty, something of a ludicrous if not vulgar whim.

The theater of the Iranian diaspora is just beginning to commence. The Revolution, at both its immediate material and extended ideological configurations, will loom largely on the dramaturgical preoccupations of the artists creating for their misplaced audience. If certain relocations of the Iranian cultural motifs had anticipated the Revolution, then certain misplaced loyalties are succeeding it. The old regime carried its self-contradictions too much towards a pseudo-rational, semi-modern, and quasi-liberated ideology. The Islamic Republic seeks to institutionalize the overpoliticized public pieties at the terrible cost of transfiguring cultural mores into bureaucratic regulations. "The Ministry of Guidance" is an Orwellian nightmare. The reaction of the diaspora, however, to the degree that it is unanimous and reveals a cultural rather than a merely political disposition, is just an implication of such dislocations of traditional loyalties that are believed to have been instrumental in the nature and outcome of the Revolution. That a sensible man should turn ass, or an atheist woman God, are symptomatics of such dislocations. But the true metamorphosis, operative at both cultural and psychological levels, is still to unfold itself. What the particulars of that complete unfolding would be still remains to be seen. But if the tragi-comedy of this husband-turned-ass is any indication, Jacques' prediction in Shakespeare's *As You Like It* (II, vi: 45-51) is not too much of a remote hint:

If it do come to pass

That any man turn ass,
Leaving his wealth and ease
A stubborn will to please,
Ducdame, ducdame, ducdame.
Here shall he see gross fools as he. . . .

THE REX CINEMA TRIAL

If there is an element of comic relief that controls the Wife's misdirected seriousness about herself in *The Ass*, there is no such redeeming factor of anxiety-control in *The Rex Cinema Trial*. This is the epitome, the final insignia, of tragedy. Some three hundred odd people—men, women, and children—perish in a fire, deliberately set to a movie house to advance a revolutionary cause. The mockery of a trial that succeeded it, and which is at the basis of this play, pales and fades in the face of the tragic weight of imagining real people burning in a deliberate fire.

Sayyad forces the Iranian diaspora, the other half of Iranians inside, to look at the mirror of their own making. Stupidity, hypocrisy, shamelessness, and a fundamental negation of something remotely human about our existence are the elements with which Sayyad chooses to have his audience in exile face itself. A revolution reveals the best and the worst in a people. A revolution is a deep and disturbing moment of anxiety for a nation. In that moment, which may last even ten years or more, a people reveal much about their collective miseries and common anxieties. What difference does it make at what side of the ideological fence the particulars of an audience stand? It is useless and misguided to resort to any construction of "they" did that to "us." A revolution is a mirror that a people hold in front of themselves. Particular actors, or opposite sides of the dividing ideological fence, are irrelevant.

But central to the enduring significance of *The Rex Cinema Trial* are the cameras of the Director who is summoned to serve the revolutionary cause despite himself. Art can either be subservient to the ideological cause or subversive to it. Whatever the historical and excusing exigencies, the Director has decided to put his craftsmanship at the disposal of the successful Revolution. Morality has no place in this. Indignation carries no clout. It is the dehumanizing impact of a mass revolution that is at the heart of a talented Director being used for propaganda purposes. Demagoguery is always the final winner in games people play with politics—reactionary or revolutionary. The innocence of Hossein Takbeʿali Zadeh, oddly enough, is the only sign of salvation in this tragedy. The Director turns out to be a self-righteous opportunist after all. His pseudo-intellectuality saves him from any rash act of sentimental orientation. Perhaps here Sayyad has personal axes to grind, perhaps a "docu-drama" is the ultimate form of ficiton, but the inarticulated innocence of the actual arsonist, an inarticulation that can only resort to the sparrow's song, that is a moving paradox on which rests the salvation of this play. For the salvation of the mobilized mass, its own mute sense of shame will have to suffice. As much as the Wife in *The Ass* is self-righteous and in a permanent accusative case, Takbeʿali Zadeh in *The Rex Cinema Trial* is innocent and noble in character. How can a woman who has her finger on all the right problems of her time be so wrong in imagining a distance between herself and others? And how can an arsonist who is responsible for the deaths of hundreds of people manage to reflect an innocent and ennobling character? The paradox must be related to this relentless gaze that the Iranian diaspora has to cast upon its own extended shadow—following it from the old to the new country.

That the events described in *The Rex Cinema Trial* are based on an actual burning of a movie-house and its subsequent trial, that this is a "docu-drama" of disturbing realism cannot add to or subtract from the intensity of tragedy as it is captured in this play. Art has a reality *sui generis*. As such, the anxieties *The Rex Cinema Trial* creates are more disturbing than those engendered by the actual news of the actual event. After the event itself, one can hope to escape the atrocities of a brutal revolution. But after seeing *The Rex Cinema Trial*, one wonders if one can ever completely regain the possibility of a genuine laughter to be occasioned by a theatrical parody of life. There is a lingering terrible aftertaste that remains perhaps permanently with the audience of *The Rex Cinema Trial*.

Such public self-flagellations are endemic to a culture of post-revolutionary exile. It denies itself laughter. It tends to get "philosophical" about life. *The Rex Cinema Trial* is a massive orchestration of disgust, of anger, of bitter disappointment, a self-condemnation for merely being human. It even does not apologize for being human. It keeps the cold-blooded murder of hundreds of innocent people at the center stage of a collective imagination, and then asks what is left worth looking at. Only a culture of post-revolutionary exile is capable of such relentless denial of anything remotely redeeming in the act of collective remembrance.

But still there is something equally relentless about man's enchantment with the world. Sayyad wrote *Samad Returns from War* after he had written and staged *The Rex Cinema Trial*. The idea, in fact, occurred to him in the course of a casual conversation. It was in April 1988 when he and I participated in a *Taʿziyeh* conference, of all things, in Hartford, Connecticut. Between two lectures, we went to get a cup of coffee. "Maybe," he said out of nowhere as we wandered into a deserted kitchen, "I should write something about Samad's coming back from the War." I cannot even remember what exactly prompted the idea. When I saw him again in Los Angeles in the following November, he had already written a draft of the play. But he lost that draft in the course of that MESA conference. He subsequently rewrote and staged *Samad Returns from War*. Peter Chelkowski and I saw the play in

New York. In it Samad was as jubilant and defiant as ever. A bit older perhaps, his movements noticeably less agile, his face a touch valanced since I saw him last in my own childhood in Iran. Yet he was heartily welcomed by the cheerful crowd: My generation remembered him well; there were younger laughers too. We were all happy to see him well, the old friend, Sayyad and Samad.

Hamid Dabashi
Columbia University

Parviz Sayyad

The Ass

A Tragi-Comedy in Three Acts

Translated from the Persian with Annotations by

Hamid Dabashi

THE ASS

Characters:

THE WIFE

THE HUSBAND

THE BROTHER

THE FATHER

THE LAWYER

THE PHYSICIAN

THE WRITER

Note

The playwright suggests that all the male characters be acted by one actor.

Act I
Scene One

Curtain up. Nighttime. Complete darkness. Sounds of shooting can be heard not too far away in the distance. A dim light is on a small garden in the courtyard. In the garden there is a single dead tree and a few pots of geraniums. THE WIFE, in her night-robe, comes and sits at the corner of the garden. She plays with the petals of the geraniums.

THE WIFE: Mother? I couldn't sleep. I came here to talk to you. He's talking again about going back to work, resuming his former job. His behavior has changed since they sent him that letter saying they needed him. He doesn't complain anymore. He's not opposed to anyone or anything. The bullets that shatter the peace in the streets don't bother him. He's quite content; he eats too much; he even snores now, something he never did before. Especially tonight, his snoring sounded like the snorting of an animal. But it was useless. Here I am.

[*Sounds of shooting with machine guns are repeated. THE WIFE listens. Pause.*]

At night, when I look from my window at other houses, I see darkness everywhere, and the windows are all closed tight. But I am sure that others have insomnia like me, or, if they sleep, they have nightmares. It's only my husband who snores. It's difficult to believe that the man who is now snoring is the same man I have loved and shared my life with for seven years. Could it be that all of his ideals, his sensitivities, aspirations, all that pride and self-determination, were pretensions? But that's impossible. My very speech, every step I took, my vision, everything, all were shaped by him. I have come to know life with him and through his eyes. How can I believe so much change in him?

A few days ago I was telling him about one of my former classmates, a seventeen-year-old girl killed in a demonstration. They told her that she had been in contact with foreign agents. I was telling him how the mother, fearing for her other children, spat on her daughter's corpse. I was telling him about this when I realized he had gone to another room. I went after him to see what could be more important than what I was telling him. He was thumbing through a journal. An idiotic journal we never even considered reading before.

[*A sound from the inside of the house brings her back to her senses.*]

I must go, mother. There are too many painful stories. I still have things to tell you.

Act I
Scene Two

Morning. THE HUSBAND and THE WIFE have just finished their breakfast in the small courtyard of the house. THE HUSBAND is hidden behind the newspaper. He is reading and cannot be seen. THE WIFE is clearing the table. In the background there is a door that opens into the building.

THE HUSBAND [*laughing*]: They have killed five more.

THE WIFE: And you laugh?

THE HUSBAND: You see, they are killing off those who brought them to power.

THE WIFE: And you laugh?

THE HUSBAND: This shows they recognize their friends from their enemies.

THE WIFE: Is that so?

THE HUSBAND: As the saying goes: "The enemy of my enemy is my friend.

[*Pause.*]

THE WIFE: Since the day they asked you to return to work, you rationalize everything, even murder. Now you talk about "necessity" and "recognition," as long as you happen to dislike the people they kill.

[*She goes into the house with some of the dishes.*]

THE HUSBAND: I didn't say killing these people is right or wrong.

[*He sets the newspaper aside. Now we see that from the neck up he is an ass.*]

All I meant was they know who's most dangerous to them: those who worked for the previous regime or their functionaries and rivals.

[*He picks up the newspaper again.* THE WIFE *returns to collect the remaining dishes.*]

I would also like to point out that I did not wish to go back to work; I have been asked to.

THE WIFE: Yes. Because they need you. As soon as they can replace you, they'll dismiss you again. You may forget you were a prominent figure in the old regime; they won't.

THE HUSBAND: When they don't want us anymore, we leave.[1]

[*While still turning the pages of the newspaper, he walks towards the building.*]

THE WIFE: That's exactly the point. When they don't want you, you leave; when they don't want you, you go. Why weren't you so conciliatory before they asked you to go back to work? Was it just a fad to be irreconcilable?

THE HUSBAND: To tell you the truth, I was stubborn because you wanted me to be. You have always wanted to make a hero out of me, but, for heaven's sake, I'm an ordinary man. I have always been.

[*He goes into the house.*]

THE WIFE: Not always. You used to say you were different from others. You showed me that you were different from your breed, that you didn't want to make a housewife out of me: a servile and obedient wife.

[*THE WIFE takes what she has collected into the house. There are a few moments of silence. Then there is a sound of something falling down and breaking, after which the horrified WIFE runs into the courtyard. A few moments later THE HUSBAND sticks his head out the door. THE WIFE turns and looks at him. Her eyes are full of terror as she sees he has an ass's head.*]

THE HUSBAND: What's going on?

[*THE WIFE holds her mouth, lest she should cry out.*]

I said what's going on?

THE WIFE: Why. . . ! What has happened to you?

THE ASS

THE HUSBAND: Eh?

THE WIFE: Why . . . sh . . . you have changed?

THE HUSBAND: Changed? I haven't changed!

THE WIFE: You have! Your head!

THE HUSBAND: My head?

THE WIFE: Your ears!

THE HUSBAND: What about my ears?

THE WIFE: You mean you don't know?

THE HUSBAND: What don't I know? What's going on?

THE WIFE: What can I say? Go and look in the mirror.

> [*THE HUSBAND goes inside. THE WIFE sits down. She holds her head and impatiently squirms in the seat.*]

Oh my God!

THE HUSBAND [*with a mirror in his hand*]: So? I don't see anything unusual.

THE WIFE: You don't? Don't you see what you have turned into?

THE HUSBAND: Turned into? What do you mean?

THE WIFE: What do I mean?

THE HUSBAND: Yes, what do you mean? What do you think has happened to me?

THE WIFE: Are you playing tricks?

THE HUSBAND: No, *you* are playing tricks.

THE WIFE [*shouting*]: Your head! Your head! It's not your own head anymore.

THE HUSBAND: Whose head is it then?

THE WIFE: The head of an animal. The head of. . . .

THE HUSBAND [*coming close to her*]: Come off it now. . . .

THE WIFE: No! Don't come near me! [*Escaping him in horror.*] Don't touch me!

THE HUSBAND: What's wrong with you?

THE WIFE: My God, he asks what's wrong with *me*! [*She begins to cry.*]

THE HUSBAND: Calm down! [*Comes to her side.*] Now look at me.

THE WIFE [*crying in horror*]: No! [*Pulls herself away.*]

THE HUSBAND: Don't torture yourself. Look at me calmly and tell me what's wrong with you.

THE WIFE: There's nothing wrong with *me*. *You*. *You*. *You* have changed.

THE HUSBAND: Okay. Tell me what's different. How have I changed?

THE WIFE: When the mirror can't tell you, what can I say?

THE HUSBAND: Okay. Come, let's look together. Maybe there is something wrong with the mirror; it may not reflect properly.

> [*THE WIFE surreptitiously looks at the mirror which THE HUSBAND is now holding in front of both of their faces.*]

THE WIFE [*murmuring*]: It's horrifying!

THE HUSBAND: What?

THE WIFE: Your head!

THE HUSBAND [*touching his head*]: My head?

THE WIFE [*touches the head and the ears of her husband with horror and moans*]: My G . . . o . . . d!

THE ASS

THE HUSBAND [*suddenly grabs her wrist*]: Tell me what's going on?

THE WIFE [*screams*]: You've turned into an ass.

THE HUSBAND: I've turned into a what?

THE WIFE: An ass. An ass.

[*Silence.*]

THE HUSBAND [*calmly*]: What do you mean I've turned into an ass?

THE WIFE: I mean you've turned into an ass.

THE HUSBAND: Are you serious?

THE WIFE: Yes.

THE HUSBAND: Do you mean a real ass or . . . or you just meant it . . . eh . . . figuratively?

THE WIFE: No, I mean a real ass.

THE HUSBAND: Perhaps you think I'm doing something foolish, and you're calling me an ass!?

THE WIFE: No, I wish it was something like that, but, and I'm sorry I have to repeat this, you have absolutely physically become an ass, that is, from the neck up.

THE HUSBAND: From the neck up.

THE WIFE: Yes, from the neck up.

THE HUSBAND: An absolute ass.

THE WIFE: An absolute physical ass.

THE HUSBAND: I see! [*Pause.*] So, to your exalted highness this humble servant looks like an ass.[2]

THE WIFE: My dear! The problem is not "to your exalted highness" or anything nonsensical like that. This is not something that I'm imagining.

I can feel you. [*She touches him again and is repulsed.*] Look! Look at the size of your ears! Your muzzle and your nose are sticking out of your neck. I mean, don't you think I can recognize an ass?!

THE HUSBAND: Yes, of course. Of course. Obviously you can. Of course you can.

[*He goes to the phone.*]

THE WIFE [*shuddering*]: It's strange I haven't had a heart attack. Oh God, I hope my own skin is not getting thick too. What are you doing?

THE HUSBAND: I'm making a phone call.

THE WIFE: To whom?

THE HUSBAND: To the doctor.

THE WIFE: What for?

THE HUSBAND: To ask him to come over. To see what's going on. To examine. . . .

THE WIFE: To examine what?

THE HUSBAND: Me! You! There must be something wrong with one of us, I suppose. Don't you think so?

THE WIFE: Wait. Please wait. This isn't an ordinary matter.

THE HUSBAND: Of course it's not. That's why we have to call the doctor.

THE WIFE: No. It's much more important than that. This is not whooping cough we have here, or pneumonia. No one has fallen down the steps and broken a bone, you see. What do you want to say to the doctor? That I'm going mad? What should I tell him? That you've turned into an ass? How can we so simply discuss this matter with an outsider? Even a doctor?

[*She takes the phone from her husband.*]

THE HUSBAND: So what do you think we should do? You're claiming that from the neck up I'm an ass.

THE WIFE: I'm not "claiming" anything. You are an ass.

THE HUSBAND: Okay. Suppose I am! Should I be persuaded or not, before I become an ass from the neck down too?!

THE WIFE: If you want to make a joke of this. . . .

THE HUSBAND: No. I'm quite serious.

THE WIFE: All right. Let's think about it. We can always call the doctor in a few minutes. But I know what you're thinking. You think I am going crazy, and that I am hallucinating. Fine. Let's suppose you're right and let's say I am imagining all this. Give me some time. Perhaps this illusion will soon go away, and I'll see you as you usually are. Come sit here, over here [*she makes her husband sit down*], and don't look at me as if I am going mad or something. I may very well go crazy soon enough. But now, at this moment, my mind is working perfectly well. Please look the other way. I can't bear the way you are staring at me.

THE HUSBAND [*angry*]: If you can't stand me looking at you . . . there isn't anything I can do. "Don't look at me." "Look the other way." I don't believe this!

THE WIFE: Don't be angry, dear. You're right. I shouldn't look at you. I won't. Here, see? I'm looking the other way. But please don't take this as a sign of insensitivity on my part. As a matter of fact, at this strange and incredible moment, more than at any other time since I've known you, I . . . pity you. . . .

THE HUSBAND: Don't feel sorry for me. I'm not the one who needs consolation.

THE WIFE: All right, but if I don't look at you, it's not that I don't want to see your face, and it's not that I don't like you. But I can't concentrate. And if. . . .

THE HUSBAND: What are you philosophizing about? Just tell me what you want to say outright, as if I don't know that all this nonsense is because of my going back to work. Thank God it's the first day, and it doesn't matter if I go in late. But I will go to work anyway, even if you think I'm a green-headed gorilla, let alone an ass.

THE WIFE [*she tries to ignore him and concentrate on what she wants to say*]: I . . . saw a movie. . . . I can't remember it's name now. A man wanted to get rid of his wife; he wanted to send her to a sanitarium so he could live with his mistress . . . so he played dead.³ But his ghost kept popping up all over the house. One day his body was rising from the pool, another day his widow thought she saw him in the bathtub. . . . All this was intended to drive the poor woman crazy. Now, of course, I don't see any reason why you should want to do the same to me. . . . However, if you wish to scare me or drive me crazy, I'd rather you put a mask on your head. . . .

THE HUSBAND: Rather than. . . .

THE WIFE: Rather than be transfigured into . . . this animal that I won't name.

THE HUSBAND [*mockingly*]: Oh . . ., I am very grateful to you for being considerate enough not to mention it! But I have not been transfigured into an animal, that is to say, I have not been transformed into a new animal. I am the same animal as I was before, and I don't have any mask on my head. I am telling you this seriously, no matter what change you think you see. It's all an illusion, a mental distortion on your part! I apologize for telling you this, but I have no other choice. So before it gets worse. . . .

[*THE HUSBAND again goes towards the phone; THE WIFE prevents him.*]

THE WIFE: No! I beg you! Sit down! I beg you to give me a few more minutes. Let's first figure out what's happening to us. [*She makes him sit down.*]

THE HUSBAND: What a day!

[*THE WIFE, who is now behind THE HUSBAND's chair, suddenly grabs his head with all her force and tries to pull off the ass mask. They struggle and both fall on the ground.*]

THE HUSBAND: What are you doing? You're pulling off my ears! You're hurting my neck!

THE WIFE: I apologize.

THE ASS

THE HUSBAND: Apologize! What's getting into you today?

THE WIFE [*murmuring*]: It's horrifying! It's horrifying, but it's true! There is no denying it.

THE HUSBAND [*mockingly*]: There is no denying what?!

THE WIFE: You're not wearing a mask!

THE HUSBAND: Well, thank God you finally accept what I've been saying all along.

THE WIFE: You have really turned into it.

THE HUSBAND: Turned into it?! Turned into what?

THE WIFE: An ass! A-S-S! An ass!

THE HUSBAND: Thank you! [*Pause.*] It's not important what you call me. I'm going back to work now. The country needs me.

THE WIFE: Ha! Ha! Ha!

THE HUSBAND: Yes! Ha! Ha! Ha! You can laugh now.

THE WIFE: That's exactly right. To do an ass's work there is always need for the likes of you. But you mean the government, not the country. You're responding to the need of the government.

THE HUSBAND: Governments change; what remains constant is the country.

THE WIFE: Governments change! Yes; and what doesn't change is the government's insurmountable need to saddle the people. It's the nature of governments. And the thing that never changes in us—except for death, delivering it from one generation to another—is the condition of being saddled. There are always enduring reasons why the government saddles the people and why the people need to be saddled: the country, the homeland, the motherland, take this and it leads you back to the beginning of history! Aren't these your own words?

THE HUSBAND: One can and must reconsider one's views. No one and nothing is absolutely perfect. Do you think you are perfect? There are hundreds of significant and insignificant things wrong with you. Just last night, in the garden, you were talking to your mother's ghost. Don't deny it now!

THE WIFE [*angrily*]: I don't deny it. But why do you have to mention it? I have told you repeatedly that my conversations with her are a completely private matter. Please don't refer to them again, and don't make it sound as if I'm crazy. Besides, if someone talks to herself when she's alone—or, as you say, to her mother's ghost—it's not a sign of anything.

THE HUSBAND: Sure, of course, there is absolutely nothing wrong with you! But everything is wrong with me, isn't it? Well then, I can improve myself, can't I? I mean, I can improve. Don't you think so?

THE WIFE: That's right!

THE HUSBAND: One way of reaching perfection is to reach oneself!

THE WIFE: Which you have.

THE HUSBAND: Let's see. Are you still insisting on what you said about me before?

THE WIFE: What?

THE HUSBAND: Those changes you claimed . . . you know, from the neck up.

THE WIFE: Of course. Don't you see me rubbing my eyes constantly? Blinking all the time? Perhaps a miracle would happen, and I'd see you again as you used to be? But it won't happen. No matter how I look at you, from whatever angle, you've changed. Had it not been from the fear of embarrassment, I would have asked our neighbors over immediately so that they could take a look at you too.

THE HUSBAND [*restlessly*]: Why don't we do that? I'll do it myself right now. . . . Oh. . . .

THE WIFE [*preventing him*]: No. Be quiet! [*Threatening.*] One person, just one person, sees you like I do, and it would be impossible for us to live together anymore. If you want to do that, go right ahead and shout!

THE HUSBAND: What do you want me to do then? Someone has to solve this problem.

THE WIFE: Before anyone does anything, I'd like to wait for a while. At least for a few hours, so if this is, as you say, my illusion, perhaps it will disappear by itself.

[*Pause. THE HUSBAND paces for a while around the courtyard.*]

THE HUSBAND: I say! If I'm an ass, I would have to be heehawing, wouldn't I? Why, then, am I able to talk to you?

THE WIFE: How do I know? Perhaps you'll soon forget how to talk too? I apologize, but you're not yet completely an ass.

THE HUSBAND: Thank God for that! [*Pause.*] Well, why don't we call the doctor? He's our friend, isn't he?

THE WIFE: He's more your friend than mine. Let's suppose he comes over. I'm sure he'll say that the cause of all this is, as you say, my mental illusion. He would want to send me to a sanitarium. Is that what you want? Are you fed up with me?

THE HUSBAND: I won't say another word. Whatever you wish. [*He sits on the edge of the table.*]

THE WIFE: Please, promise me you won't leave the house today, and in a few hours, if our situation has not changed, we'll go to someone. But in choosing this person we have to be very careful. This could turn into a scandal.

THE HUSBAND: Okay. But who, for example? You choose!

THE WIFE: Let me ask my brother for help.

THE HUSBAND [*furious*]: Him?! You want to tell him?! What do you want to tell him?! That I've become an ass? You want to tell a mule that I've become an ass?!

THE WIFE: Don't insult my brother! After all, he's closer to me than anyone else.

THE HUSBAND: And how are you going to find him anyway? If he could be found, he would be dead ten times over by now.

THE WIFE: Let me worry about that.

THE HUSBAND: No! I'd rather trot to the stable and heehaw than permit someone like him to pass judgment on us. If he were a good judge, before anything else, he would have judged his own actions.

THE WIFE: Just because he is my brother. . . .

THE HUSBAND: No! I'll solve this problem my own way. Without going to the doctor or seeing anyone else who knows you and me. I'll go back to work. [*He stands up.*] The first person in the street who says that I'm an ass or who looks at me in a peculiar way, I'll immediately come back home. . . .

[*He goes into the building.*]

THE WIFE [*angry*]: What home? There won't be any home. Why don't you understand?

THE HUSBAND [*comes out wearing his jacket*]: No home? How about a stable, then? I'm an ass, aren't I?

[*Taking a comb out of his pocket, THE HUSBAND disappears. THE WIFE suddenly thinks of something, goes inside the building. The sound of closing and locking a door is heard.*]

THE WIFE'S VOICE: You're not going anywhere.

THE HUSBAND'S VOICE: Open the door! Right this second! I'm telling you, open the door!

THE WIFE'S VOICE: No! You're staying here until I come back.

THE HUSBAND'S VOICE: I'm warning you, open the door!

THE WIFE'S VOICE: I'm going to lock all the doors. Even if you break this one down, you won't get out through the others. Calm down, dear! Just for one day be my prisoner. Give me a chance to figure this thing out.

THE ASS 19

[*THE WIFE reappears. She is dressed to go out and has a scarf on her head. She stays close to the door behind which THE HUSBAND is locked.*]

Forgive me. I love you.

[*Pause. Going out, she slows down near the geranium pot and abruptly sits down.*]

Mother! Something terrible has happened, so terrible that I can't even tell *you*! I know you see everything, and right now you know what has happened to me. What I mean is, I can't bring myself to actually say it. At least for now. You have to forgive me, but to find my brother, I have to talk to his mother—your rival wife. I know talking to her is to do you wrong,[4] but I have no other choice. Only she can tell me where he is. Please understand my pitiful situation. I know you are kind enough to forgive your wretched daughter.

[*The curtain comes down as THE WIFE exits.*]

Act II
Scene One

THE WIFE is visiting her BROTHER. The stage is set to look like a basement, or a storage room. THE BROTHER wears a military jacket, very similar to those worn by guerrillas. He has a thick mustache. He is lacing his military boots.

THE BROTHER: To tell you the truth, I really don't know what to say. When I wanted to intervene in your private life, you didn't let me. Now, you want me to come and judge what has happened to you and your husband. But nobody's private life interests me anymore.

THE WIFE: Not even mine?

THE BROTHER: Not even yours. Especially not yours. I have lost many sisters, my dear sister. Younger than you, and more deserving to live than you. Innocent girls, in the prime of their lives. I feel I am responsible to them and to their miseries. I feel no responsibility towards you. You stand aside and philosophize about all this mad-house we call our country just to secure your own wretched ends.

THE WIFE: You have to feel responsible for the life and death of those young girls—boys too, which you fail to mention. You know very well that you're guilty for the loss of their lives, whether you like it or not, whether you admit it or not. [*Pause.*] Look who is feeling sorry for the young and their perished youth. The rotten seeds of your infested plants blossom only in the soil of youth. It would not blossom in harder and more solid earth. It's difficult to send a forty-year-old man to the front, but it's even more difficult to have him killed in public demonstrations. Change the conscription age from twenty to thirty and, mark my words, there won't be any army or any war. It's the adventurous nature, the thoughtless and naive emotions of the young people that can be used for seizing power. You are a vampire, you always seek your prey among the young. You feed the marrow of your bones with the raw and invigorating blood of their youth. My dear brother, you couldn't care less about anybody, and I mean anybody, but yourself. Some day in the future the newspapers will write: "Those innocent youths who perished in the battle-fields laid down their lives for their beliefs." But the fact is that those beliefs were injected into them, forced onto them. They were made to take root and grow, so that you and the likes of you could be victorious and powerful. And now you say you feel responsible for them? Oh! I am really impressed! Well you ought to feel responsible. You send them to their death! You are responsible for their blood being shed, to the very last drop!

THE BROTHER: And you think I do it for prestige and position? Ha?! To seize power?

THE WIFE: Precisely!

THE BROTHER: But I could have had power before this—as you call it—gamble. Couldn't I? Didn't they offer me positions and prestige?

THE WIFE: Yes. But it wasn't enough for you. My dearest brother, more than anybody else, I know you from the inside out. You wanted more than was possible. The positions that would satisfy you were either non-existent—so you had to have them created—or they were above you. Presidency? Ha! Ha! Ha! Joint Chief of Staff? Well, that wouldn't fit your image. Prime Minister or maybe a minister? No, not the type. Member of the parliament or a governor? But so many people were in line for these posts ahead of you that you would have died before your turn came up. Of course, there were lower positions available, positions that many of your fellow-travelers accepted—and still do. The fact of the matter is, my dearest brother, that for the likes of you it's either all or nothing. This time the only possibility was "nothing."

[*Pause.*]

THE BROTHER: How interesting! So that's how you see me? A criminal!

THE WIFE: Precisely. Of course, you can call yourself a hero, you can even have others call you that.

THE BROTHER: I don't care about others. But you know I don't call myself a hero.

THE WIFE: Well, I said that others would do it for you. The miserable things need it. But don't pretend that it bothers you. You do accept a title that you don't deserve.

THE BROTHER: If you call self-sacrifice and honorable struggle against tyranny and demagoguery a crime, then what do you call murder in the name of establishing tyranny and demagoguery?

THE WIFE: Crime!

THE BROTHER: Crime? So they are criminal, and we are criminal too! And there is no difference between us?

THE WIFE: No. They are more criminal than you, that's all. Of course, this is the case now. Because they have more power and more weapons, so they can kill more of you. But when your gang comes to power—to the same power that your opponents have—then we will see who kills more.

THE BROTHER: We kill in order not to get killed. We kill for an ideal that is exactly the opposite of their demagoguery. These are different in principle.

THE WIFE: But practically the same. Besides, they have also killed—and are still killing—with the same excuse as yours, and under the same slogan. Any other group that is willing to kill for its ideals can rationalize its crimes in precisely the same way.

THE BROTHER: Is this why you came to see me? What can a criminal like me do for you? Besides, even if I could help you, why do you come to a criminal for help?

THE WIFE; I came here not because, unfortunately, you are my brother but because I know your shortcomings; and because of that I don't hesitate to reveal a deficiency of my own to you. And I am not asking for a big favor either. I simply want you to come over tonight and see my husband.

THE BROTHER: Whatever for?

THE WIFE: Just to see him. To see whether he is the same creature that he used to be.

THE BROTHER: Without seeing him I can guess that he has certainly gone back to his origin. Recent events have revealed the true nature of many people. So far as your husband is concerned, I must say I always knew his true nature: a wretched liberal-bourgeois to his bones; although he always pretended to agree with your anarchist and radical views, just to get you to marry him. Individualism! Superior-man! Super-Human! And all that bullshit a la what's-his-name, that bearded English whoremonger.[5] And then the natural desire for copulation or the tendency towards marriage—what you bourgeois call love—made you encourage his pretensions and pomposities.

THE WIFE: Well, you may be right about him to a certain extent, but I don't want you to come and talk to him or convince him to do anything. I want you to come and see if his appearance has changed at all, you know?

THE BROTHER: I still don't have the faintest idea of what you're talking about?

THE WIFE: His head! His face! I want you to see whether it's like it was before. To me he looks very different.

THE BROTHER: In what way?

THE WIFE: I can't say. I want you to see for yourself. I don't want to give you any pre-conceived idea. Please come. Just look at him for a few minutes. Tell me what you see and then go. . . . That's all.

[*Pause.*]

THE BROTHER: I see. Well, this could very well be a plot . . . to capture me . . . or to take me where. . . .

[*Pause.*]

THE WIFE: Is that what you think? [*She starts to leave.*] I don't want you to come.

THE BROTHER: Sorry. I apologize.

THE WIFE; You idiot! If I wanted to report you, would I endanger myself by coming here? I would have sent them to get you. [*Pause.*] Is this the intelligence with which you want to lead the people?

THE BROTHER: I told you I'm sorry. Look, I can't tell you what time I'll come, but I will try. If I am alive, I'll be there tonight.

THE WIFE; With my luck, they'll get you before you can help me.

THE BROTHER: Well, for that matter, forget that you saw me here. I will not stay here anymore. Wherever I am found no longer remains a safe place for me.

THE WIFE: At any rate, whether you come or not, whether you are here or not, I will not come to see you again. [*She leaves.*]

THE BROTHER: That suits me fine. Tell mother not to send me unwelcome guests. Tell her to forget about me, to leave me alone.

THE WIFE [*comes back*]: I almost forgot, I promised her I'd give you a message from her in exchange for her telling me where you are.

THE BROTHER: Spit it out.

THE WIFE: She said: If you are really fighting for the "wretched masses," then I too am a wretched person, aren't I? How more wretched could I be? I have lost two of my sons in less than six months? Don't do anything rash and foolish! I don't want to lose the only son I have left. Not only am I your mother, I am a member of the "wretched masses" too.

[*Pause.*]

THE BROTHER: Is that all?

THE WIFE: Do you have any message to comfort her?

THE BROTHER: Oh yes. . . .

THE WIFE: What?

THE BROTHER: Fuck off.

[*Blackout.*]

Act II
Scene Two

A room in THE FATHER's house. Wearing his religious gown and yarmulke, THE FATHER is saying his prayers. THE WIFE is sitting on a small trunk.

THE WIFE: Lucky you, father! Lucky, indeed! After all these years, you're still bending and bowing[6] so earnestly to something you even don't know what it is. Lucky you, indeed! Believing so wholeheartedly that there is another world. How come you are so faithful and I so faithless? How come what you call "the ray" or "certitude" shines on your heart and not on mine? Doesn't that prove that there isn't any light at all? Shouldn't light illuminate; should it not illuminate equally, no matter what or whom? [*Pause.*] But never mind; keep on praying! If only that light would illuminate my heart too!? If only that light were not so selective in its illumination!?

THE FATHER [*who has just finished saying his prayers*]: "I seek forgiveness from God." You never come to see me, and when you come you bring me sacrilege. Aren't you ashamed? [*He collects his prayer rug.*] What brings you here?

THE WIFE: I have come to see *you*, father. [*She pronounces "father" sarcastically.*] It never occurs to you to come and see how your daughter is doing, does it?

THE FATHER: When God forgets about someone, so do His obedient servants.

THE WIFE: Has your selfish God told you to face Him and forget about your children?

THE FATHER: Children? What children? I had only one child, and he was sacrificed to God. How lucky he was! He has joined the Almighty. He is always in the pure presence of the Almighty. Ah! To face God....

THE WIFE: They say when Abraham was about to sacrifice his son Ishmael,[7] God pitied him and sent Gabriel to give him a lamb to sacrifice instead. Apparently God is not as kind as He used to be, since we continue to sacrifice thousands of children to Him and He couldn't care less.

THE FATHER: Death is inevitable. "Lo! We are Allah's and lo! unto Him we are returning."[8] Death is inevitable.

THE WIFE: That's right. To you and your kind death is inevitable, not life.

THE FATHER: This sinful life that you and your kind lead, it amounts to nothing compared to God's majesty.

THE WIFE: Then why do you cling to it like a leech? If life is so worthless, why have you forged so many guardians on it? So many prophets, Imams, leaders, muftis, sultans, governors, prayer-leaders, clerics, custodians, guardians, militias? Aren't all these to meddle with the same worthless lives of people just to make a fortune? Forty thousand thugs to govern this worthless life? Wow! The fact of the matter is that you are all liars! You always have been!

> You preach to people to denounce the world
> But you make your own bundle of silver and gold.[9]

[*THE FATHER wants to say something; but THE WIFE does not let him.*]

They put one of your sons against the wall and executed him. And who were they? The same people who sent your other son to get killed for their cause. You didn't even go to his funeral.

THE FATHER [*angrily*]: He was not my son.

THE WIFE: He was. He was, and he believed in God, too.

THE FATHER [*outraged*]: He was a hypocrite.[10] He was a hypocrite. [*To himself, crying.*] O God! Forgive us all!

THE WIFE [*calmly*]: He was a martyr for your God. Or at least the poor thing thought so. But he didn't become a martyr in a way that conformed to your interests. Your oldest son, too, is among the true believers. But if you knew his hide-out, you would report him to be killed and that would suit your interests.

THE FATHER [*affectionately*]: What are you talking about? What "interests"? Why do you say that? Thank God, I don't need any worldly possessions.

THE WIFE: That's precisely the point: worldly possessions are not enough. You want a secure niche in Paradise, too. Apparently its price is too high to be paid by today's inflationary currencies. Even gold won't do the trick. It takes blood to get to your Paradise. Fresh blood. It needs the hot blood of youth. God's thirst for blood, for sacrifice, is never completely satisfied. And you are His agent. Agents of blood.

THE FATHER [*screaming*]: Get out of here! Get out! Don't give me that pitiful nonsense that you've learned from that ass-headed husband of yours.

[*Pause.*]

THE WIFE: From whom?

THE FATHER: Your husband!

THE WIFE: Why did you call him ass-headed?

THE FATHER: Because that's what he is, isn't he?

THE WIFE: Have you seen him recently?

THE FATHER: God forbid. I don't need to see him. Any man who teaches such nonsense to his wife must be ass-headed. No doubt about that.

[*Pause.*]

THE WIFE: I see. And why do you think only men can teach their wives something? When will you get it through your thick skull that women have absolutely no less intelligence than men? It's men who have been the cause of all calamity in history. It's men who have filled the world with injustice and tyranny.

THE FATHER: And who forced man out of Paradise?

THE WIFE: Woman! Woman! She led him out of an artificial and worthless paradise to show him real life. But what did he do in return? Instead of using his physical force, which itself is a primary injustice, to modify the injustice of nature, he multiplied it. He repressed his own mate, his wife. He made his wife, who was weaker than him, into a slave. The more our mothers gave birth, the more our fathers killed. They began to compete with each other to kill what the mothers had given birth to. Like the male fish in the sea who take turns behind the pregnant female fish, eating every fetus that comes out. But our species had to go one step further than any of the others. Man completed his selfish and tyrannical game by inventing male gods, male prophets, male leaders, and this continues to this very day, and it will continue until the last day.

THE FATHER: What do you want from my life? What are you doing here?

THE WIFE: I told you, I have come to see you. I was depressed. I thought to come and visit the murderer who killed my mother.

[*Pause.*]

THE FATHER: What did you say? Do you think I murdered your mother? Aren't you ashamed to make such an accusation?

THE WIFE [*calmly*]: Father, I have talked to the doctor who was present when my mother was giving birth. I finally found him. He told me that my mother had a massive hemorrhage after giving birth to me. She needed a transfusion. But you didn't permit it. You wouldn't accept the charges.

THE FATHER: Do you think it was because of the cost? No! You fool! I didn't want them to give her the filthy blood of God-knows-who off the street.

THE WIFE: Nothing is filthier than your mind, father.

THE FATHER: They bring you blood and inject it into you. Who knows whose blood it is? Is it an infidel's, a Muslim's, a Christian's, or a Bahai's. . .?

THE WIFE: It wouldn't make a difference to me, father. What I wanted was my mother.

[*Feeling the intensity of his daughter's sorrow, THE FATHER retreats.*]

THE FATHER: One's life and death is not in one's own hand. It's in God's hands. He brings us into this world, and He takes us out. He gives, and He takes away.

THE WIFE: I suppose so. Let's suppose so. Let's suppose you're innocent and He is to blame.

THE ASS 31

THE FATHER: Who's to blame?

THE WIFE: God.

THE FATHER: Blame for what?

THE WIFE: Killing my mother.

THE FATHER: I seek forgiveness from God!

THE WIFE: All right, ask Him then. I don't have any relation with Him, you know. You're in contact with Him directly and indirectly a few times every day on this prayer rug. Well, ask Him then. . . .

THE FATHER [*angrily*]: Ask Him what?

THE WIFE: Why He killed her? That's what.

THE FATHER: Don't say such things, child! Bite your tongue! Do not blaspheme! You will be punished for it, I'm warning you.

THE WIFE: You mean even more?

THE FATHER: Of course. Of course. His ocean of forgiveness is as boundless as his anger. What do we know? Who are we to know? It's not for us to meddle in these things. His grand wisdom is beyond our comprehension.

THE WIFE [*heartfully*]: What tyrannical wisdom is this that won't allow me to remember my mother's face? I never had a chance to put my head on her lap even once. Or feel her kind hands caressing my hair, the simplest and most natural right of any child. It was my right, too, to have a mother, to be raised in her care, with her kindness.

[*She begins to cry.*]

THE FATHER: Dearest.

THE WIFE [*moaning*]: Nonsense? He gives and He takes away! He never gave me or my mother anything. He only took, that's all.

THE FATHER: I seek God's forgiveness!

THE WIFE: She was only nineteen years old. Only nineteen years old.

[*Approaching from behind his crying daughter,* THE FATHER *reaches out to touch her hair, but at the last moment he stops. He leaves hurriedly.* THE WIFE *cries in solitude. Blackout.*]

Act III
Scene Three

THE WIFE is in THE LAWYER's office. THE LAWYER's voice can be heard from the other room.

THE LAWYER's voice [*laughing*]: Ha, ha, ha! It's interesting, it's very interesting.

THE WIFE: Interesting?

THE LAWYER's voice: It's really interesting. Ha, ha, ha!

THE WIFE: What do you mean "interesting"? There is really no word more meaningless than "interesting." It's like a joker in a game of poker; you can use it anywhere. *You* may have some idea what you mean by it but no one else does. What do you exactly mean: "interesting"? Is it interesting positively or negatively? It is good or bad or what?

THE LAWYER [*comes out with two drinks, gives one to THE WIFE*]: Well, what word do you think I should have used?

THE WIFE: Catastrophic, painful, dreadful, incredible, or at least strange. Any other word than "interesting" defines my husband's situation. . . . What is this?

THE LAWYER: A soft drink.

THE WIFE: I should have guessed you wouldn't dare to offer me a *real* drink.[11]

THE LAWYER [*ignoring her sarcasm*]: I wasn't referring to your husband when I said it's interesting.

THE WIFE: Oh! What did you mean then?

THE LAWYER: I was thinking about my own situation.

THE WIFE: Hmmm?

THE LAWYER: I was thinking that if you had married me when I proposed to you many years ago, you would probably be seeing me today as you now see your husband! Ha, ha, ha!

THE WIFE: I see!

THE LAWYER: Of course I regret not having had the honor of being your husband. Perhaps one of the reasons that I am not married yet is because I never found anyone like you. But I am happy not to be afflicted like your husband.

THE WIFE; What do you mean--"afflicted"?

THE LAWYER: Your disliking him so much that he appears like a monster to you.

THE WIFE: Who said a monster?

THE LAWYER: Animal, what's the difference?

THE WIFE: There's a lot of difference. An ass is different from a monster.

THE LAWYER: Well, the point is you dislike him. I am sorry, but as you said yourself, he displeases you in a rather terrible way.

THE WIFE: If you imply that I don't love him anymore, you are wrong. I do love him very much. If not more than when I first met him, then at least as much.

THE LAWYER: Then why did you come here to explore the possibilities of separation and divorce?

THE WIFE: Precisely for that reason. I'm afraid that if I don't leave him, my love will turn into hatred. I have nothing to rely on in this world other than love. I don't want to lose it.

THE LAWYER: To tell you the truth, I never imagined that love could have such consequences.

THE WIFE: Oh yes, even worse than that. I'm afraid that I might kill him if he stays this way. First I'd kill him and then myself, rather than be witness to such a tragedy. I'd rather see the man I dearly love dead than transfigured.

THE ASS

THE LAWYER: It's very interesting! [*THE WIFE looks at him.*] Oh! I beg your pardon. . . . I mean it's very strange at any rate. . . . "What can I do for you?" as the English say![12]

THE WIFE: Before anything else, I'd like to know what my rights are as a woman in case I don't want to live with my husband anymore.

THE LAWYER: For what reasons?

THE WIFE: Well, simply . . . in case I don't want to.

THE LAWYER: Just because you don't want to. My dear madam, for that reason you have absolutely no rights.

THE WIFE: Absolutely none?

THE LAWYER: Absolutely none.

THE WIFE: And if my husband wanted to . . .?

THE LAWYER: If he wants, he can divorce you.

THE WIFE: Just because he wants to?

THE LAWYER: That's right.

THE WIFE: Do you think this is just?

THE LAWYER: Not at all. Not at all.

THE WIFE: How interesting!

THE LAWYER: Well, what do you mean "interesting"?

THE WIFE: I mean it's strange that even you say it's not just.

THE LAWYER: Well, how can I say that it's just when it's not?

THE WIFE: Do you say that as a human being or as a lawyer?

THE LAWYER: I don't know how you can separate the two. Hafez[13] was not a lawyer, but seven hundred years ago he said it all for everybody, including lawyers: "This world and all things in it are nothing in nothing."

[*Pause.*] See how much meaning is condensed in this very line, and then it's in the second line that his insight reaches its height: "A thousand times have I ascertained this point." He means to say: Don't get me wrong; I am not expressing a poetic opinion, a play on words; it's based on documentation, authentication, historical verification, scrutiny and research that I say this. This world and all things in it are nothing in nothing. After Hafez, my dear lady, I take my hat off to that Swiss dramatist,[14] one of whose characters comes to the front-stage and says quite candidly, "Ladies and gentlemen, let me not waste your time; there is no justice." [*Pause.*] That's it, my dear; there is absolutely no justice.

THE WIFE: And then you work for the institution of justice.

THE LAWYER: If you had said the institution of injustice, you would have put my mind at ease. It's precisely for that reason that I can accept more easily than you that there's no justice. I can accept it and feel it to the marrow of my bones. You know I was a judge for ten years. The problem occurs only when you don't believe in any justice and you are forced to pass judgment on others. I realized it was impossible for me to do so. I changed my profession and became a lawyer.

THE WIFE: What's the difference when you can't bring about any justice, when you can't do anything. What difference does it make what kind of position you have or role you play?

THE LAWYER: True. One can't bring about any justice; but that doesn't mean that one is not doing anything. You see, my dearest, the point is that one cannot be just. At best I can be not unjust, or I can commit less injustice. Thus, the best the ministry of justice—which, by the way, I call the Federal Department of Injustice—and all its branches, lawyers, and judges can do is to prevent injustice, to alleviate tyranny. But it cannot establish any justice. This is not in its power. You can't count on it. But if tyranny is alleviated, that in itself is an achievement, isn't it?

THE WIFE; Well, how can you get around this unjust law which says that even with a reason I can't divorce my husband, and that even without a reason he can divorce me?

THE LAWYER: Alas, this is a case I simply cannot do anything about. But one advantage of law is that sometimes it also points the way towards doing something illegal. I mean in such cases we may find some loopholes and discover a way out.

THE WIFE: For example?

THE LAWYER: For example, if we could prove that in principle the couple cannot go on living together.

THE WIFE: Principle? What principle?

THE LAWYER: The principles of marriage, for example. If it could be proved that the husband is impotent or absolutely incapable of providing for his wife or has contracted some contagious disease.

THE WIFE: What if they have nothing in common? What if a couple reach an intellectual and spiritual dead-end?

THE LAWYER: These things, my dearest, are not acceptable in the kinds of courts we have. They'll say the wife must tolerate the husband until he gets better. Even in cases of a contagious disease, if it's not fatal, the court will not pass a judgment in favor of the woman. I had a female client once who had a strange problem after her marriage. As soon as this lady heard her husband's voice, even on the phone, her skin would break out in a rash. This was a psychological problem, but it also had physical effects. I mean you could visibly see the red spots on the woman's skin. Despite this, I could not get her a divorce from the court. They said she had to tolerate the rash, and gradually it would go away.

THE WIFE: Did it get better?

THE LAWYER: No, dearest, it got worse. Each time the red spots got bigger and took longer to go away. Finally I had to convince the husband to file for divorce.

THE WIFE: What difference did it make who filed for divorce?

THE LAWYER: A lot of difference. The couple were madly in love with each other, and this was a problem that the woman had contracted. Morally, he was responsible for filing for the divorce. In your case, too, I think I should talk to your husband.

THE WIFE: Whatever for?

THE LAWYER: To ask him to file for divorce.

THE WIFE: And what if he doesn't accept?

THE LAWYER: If he doesn't accept, then we will think of something else.

THE WIFE: If there is a solution, why don't we offer it now? Why do we have to force him to do something unwillingly just for my sake?

THE LAWYER: There is one excuse for which we don't need his consent to get your divorce.

THE WIFE: Well?

THE LAWYER: You have to say that he is irreligious, that he is an atheist.

[*Pause.*]

THE WIFE: Do you really think I can do such a thing?

THE LAWYER: Why not? If this is your only choice and you really want to get your divorce, why not?

THE WIFE: You mean I have to sink that low to get my legal rights?

THE LAWYER [*laughing*]: Legal, shmegal, what legal rights?

THE WIFE: Natural, my natural rights.

THE LAWYER: But you are not making a false accusation. So far as I remember, your husband has never believed in God. Unless he has recently changed his mind. Has he?

THE WIFE: One has as much right to believe in a god as one has the right to believe in none. To believe or not to believe is a completely private matter and has to do with the person's choice. It has to do with an individual's inner life. I consider violating his privacy a profound disloyalty, especially in these days when no one has any right to privacy, when the individual privacy of people is not respected.

[*She rises to leave.*]

THE LAWYER: At any rate, it's no worse than your own claim that he's become an ass from the neck up.

[*Pause.*]

THE WIFE: I believed the story about your client's skin rash, didn't I?

THE LAWYER: That's different.

THE WIFE: Would you have believed it if you'd just heard about it?

THE LAWYER: If it were hearsay, probably not. But since I saw it with my own eyes, I cannot not believe what I have seen myself.

THE WIFE: Precisely. I have seen it too, with my own eyes. [*Pause.*] You can see it too if you want.

THE LAWYER: Okay. I'll see him. But I think you should also contact a physician.

[*Curtain.*]

Act II
Scene Four

THE WIFE is in THE PHYSICIAN's office. She is resting on a sofa that resembles an examination table and is looking at a geranium that is prominently located on a shelf in front of her. THE PHYSICIAN enters. He puts a tape recorder on a table next to THE WIFE and sets it on record. THE WIFE is unaware of his presence. THE PHYSICIAN coughs to announce his entrance.

THE PHYSICIAN: What were you thinking about?

THE WIFE [*pointing out the flower*]: About this. . . .

THE PHYSICIAN: It's beautiful, isn't it?

THE WIFE: Very much so.

THE PHYSICIAN: Geraniums don't need much care. They grow anywhere. They don't even need to have roots.

THE WIFE: It's rather strange you keep it in your office. It is not usually considered a decorative flower.

THE PHYSICIAN: What do I care if it's considered decorative or not. I like it anyway. It reminds me of my mother, who was very dear to me.

THE WIFE: That's strange.

THE PHYSICIAN: What?

THE WIFE: Nothing.

THE PHYSICIAN: Well, let's start. Your situation reminds me of a play I saw a few years ago where the inhabitants of a city were gradually turning into rhinoceroses. They grew horns on their foreheads and, instead of talking, they began to grunt. Have you seen it?

THE WIFE: No, I haven't seen it, but I've read it. It's *Rhinoceros* by Eugene Ionesco.

THE PHYSICIAN: That's right. The point is that before the final physical transfigurations of these people, changes began to appear in their behavior and their social relationships. My question is, before seeing your husband this morning at breakfast, did you pick up any change in his general behavior and, if so, what?

THE WIFE: Well, I guess . . . well, he's started watching television. He never watched television before; and how he is glued to it until the last frame of the last program. Sometimes all the programs are over, and I still see him staring at the black and white dots on the screen. As for the regular journals and the morning and afternoon papers, he won't put them down until he reads them all from page one to the auto ads. He used to refuse even to thumb through them.

THE PHYSICIAN: Isn't this because he has nothing else to do?

THE WIFE: But why doesn't he read books anymore? He used to have a very systematic program of reading. Why doesn't he listen to music as he used to?

THE PHYSICIAN: I haven't listened to music or picked up a good book either in a long time. In fact, because of my profession, I have to read to stay up-to-date on modern discoveries in medicine. But occasionally you don't feel like doing anything educational. You escape seriousness. In fact, you intentionally want to waste your time. It happens.

THE WIFE: I know what you mean. And I accept the fact that one can get depressed every once in a while; but I can't understand depression leading to changes in one's moral and human characteristics. You may or may not listen to music; but this is different from having two kids seeking your protection from the fear of persecution and you handing them over to the authorities rather than giving them shelter. [*Pause.*] He did that. A few weeks ago, two youngsters knocked on our door. They were barely seventeen or eighteen years old—scared to death, pale, shivering. They asked us to let them hide inside because they said they were being followed; and if they were caught, they would be killed. My husband said to them: "Get out of here . . . or I'll call the authorities and report you this instant." The boys took off. . . .

[*She cannot go on.*]

THE PHYSICIAN: He didn't hand them over, did he?

THE WIFE: What's the difference? A few minutes after they left, we heard gunshots. Even if they got away . . . in my mind they were killed. Their red blood, their young bodies, wasted on the ground.

[*She quietly weeps.*]

THE PHYSICIAN: I don't know what I would have done if I had been in his place. I can imagine, but it would have to really happen to me before I'd know how courageous I am. Perhaps he wanted to prevent a disturbing incident. Just think what would have happened if they had been shot right on your doorstep, before your eyes, or . . ., at any rate, he didn't want you to get upset. Perhaps he was thinking more of you than himself. . . .

THE WIFE [*screaming*]: No! He wasn't. He knew me. He knows me. He knows I don't need such comforts. I cried. I cried all night while he sat downstairs and watched that wretched boob tube.

[*THE PHYSICIAN waits for THE WIFE to finish crying in silence.*]

THE PHYSICIAN: The question I am about to ask you is rather personal. If you wish, you can refuse to answer it. [*Pause.*] Once you quit your job in the new regime, why didn't you leave this country? . . . At that time, it was easy to get out.

THE WIFE [*takes a long breath so she can go on*]: Are you taping me?

THE PHYSICIAN [*turns the tape recorder off*]: I'm sorry.

THE WIFE: I wanted to leave. He didn't want to. Now I know why. My brother is right about him: He is conservative and an absolute hypocrite.[15] He didn't want to abandon his house or his villa at the shore or his money in the bank—which it was then too late to send out. I begged him to leave. I told him, let's go somewhere, we'll get a job—even if it's menial—and live a humble life. I told him, let's go somewhere else, somewhere other than here. "Where you can look in the mirror and not be ashamed that you are a human being."[16] He said, "No, it will be the same everywhere." I told him no, no! There are still places where human beings have not lost all their self-respect. There are still places where you can relax after your day at work by drinking a glass of beer or sitting in a street-corner cafe with a cup of coffee and looking at people passing by. There you can feel good about yourself; at least you are not imprisoned. There are places where you can see a good show or a movie. You can go to an exhibition or a concert. You can see a ballet and see that even if *you* can't do those things, there are still people who can, that there is still hope in humanity, hope in striving in art or advancing in science; that there is still light, even if it is an artificial light, it is not a lie, you can believe in it, it's a light and it shines on you. You can see it and feel it.

[*Pause.*]

THE PHYSICIAN: Your words are very familiar to my ears. It's as if I'm listening to myself. Had it not been for my children, I would have escaped this place no matter what. But every time I tried to make a move, I realized I couldn't endanger them for my own sake. [*Pause.*] Enough is enough! One of these days, this phone will ring and nobody will answer. You know where I'll be? I'll be gone, gone.

THE WIFE: Why do you talk of leaving? Do you really want to leave?

THE PHYSICIAN: Do I want to leave? Of course I want to leave.

THE WIFE: But you are a physician.

THE PHYSICIAN: Because I'm a physician I don't have a right to live? Can't I wish for a glass of beer in a bar? Do such luxuries befit only you, just because you're not a physician?

THE WIFE: If I talk of leaving, it's to escape idleness and self-deception. By staying here and working, my husband and I are committing treason; but by leaving, you would be abandoning your duty. Your work leads to people's good health; ours only strengthens the regime. Those are two different things.

THE PHYSICIAN: You intellectuals come up with all kinds of excuses for your activity or inactivity; but you never consider them sufficient for others. Why do you think the same conditions that justify your inactivity would not justify mine? Without any trial, they executed a colleague of mine because he had helped a Kurdish guerrilla. Now if the same guerrillas get their chance, they would execute me just because I operated on this or that Mullah's hernia. Because they have forced the veil on little girls or have changed "Azar" to "Zubaydeh" in the textbooks,[17] you have retired to your home and read Goethe or Beyhaqi's *Annals*.[18] And you try to maintain a good conscience because you don't work with the regime. Well, lucky you. But I have to shut up and work, at any price and under any conditions, because, God forbid, I am a physician. [*Pause.*] They come and take away for interrogation a patient of mine whom I had put in the I.C.U. He still had an I.V. in his veins. But I have to keep on working. The next day, like a perfect moron, I have to go back at the same time to the same hospital and the same department. Why? Because I am a physician. I am on call one night as a medical examiner when they bring in the corpses of a bunch of youngsters they have just machine-gunned. Then they want me to examine them and report the number of bullet holes in their bodies. I ask them, is this the job of a medical examiner? "Revolution has its own rules," they reply. "You have to verify the number of holes in their bodies so that we can demand compensation for our bullets from their relatives." [*Pause.*] Where are you in such moments, Mr. or Mrs. Intellectual? If you are lucky and have run away, perhaps you are sipping your coffee while gazing at the eternal Champs Élysées; or if you have been left behind from the caravan of runaways, then you are reading Goethe and Beyhaqi's *Annals* at home; or you are practicing *Santur*.[19] But I have to keep practicing medicine because I am a physician.

THE WIFE: I apologize. I didn't mean to upset you.

THE PHYSICIAN: I had decided to go to one of the provinces, where it's less crowded and people know each other, respect each other, and aren't constantly at each other's throats so shamelessly. But my friends who had gone before me came back. They said the local mullahs had preached on pulpits that people should not take their wives or daughters to us physicians because it's sinful. Now the old medicine men, herbalists, and talisman-writers are following the mullahs, and gradually people are refusing to visit modern doctors. You see? People don't need us as much as you think.

THE WIFE: But you know that's not true. Isn't that enough? People are deceived. They are caught in the old talisman of ignorance and superstition. They can't understand what has happened or is happening to them. You, who know, are responsible, if not to the people and the country, then at least to your profession.

THE PHYSICIAN: Responsibility to the medical profession begins when a patient comes through this door and asks me for help. It wouldn't make a difference whether he were a Philippino or an African, an Arab Muslim or a Canadian Christian. The relationship between the patient and the physician creates responsibility; their nationality is of no importance. Consequently, as a physician, I can go anywhere and still be as useful as I would be in my own country. And that's more than I can say about you people. The point is that if we're supposed to leave, nobody is more eligible than I. That's what I'm trying to say.

THE WIFE: Well, you can go too, like others. People here don't give a damn anyway; they have their own herbalists and talisman-writers.

THE PHYSICIAN: Yes, but my problem is that I don't have the guts to do it. Like a polluted pond, I've remained still for too long. I've become stagnant. I can't find a way out. In this way, I'm like your husband. Although I don't have the slightest faith, I pontificate about how much I pity my country when I'm with my colleagues. At parties, I preach about people and my duties toward them, while I know damn well it's all a bunch of crap. That's right, I don't have the guts. To uproot myself and start all over again would take enormous courage, and I simply don't have it. I'm very much like your husband.

THE WIFE: And here I thought you are like me. What you said about the geranium made me think so. Because it reminds me of my mother too.

THE PHYSICIAN: Really?

THE WIFE: Yes. I don't know why I think my mother must have smelled like a geranium. Perhaps because it has a sad and dark red about it. It blossoms unsparingly. It's always content; and, as you say, it doesn't even need a root to grow.

THE PHYSICIAN: Do you still talk with her?

THE WIFE: With whom?

THE PHYSICIAN: With your mother?

THE WIFE: But my mother has been dead for years now. I've never seen her.

THE PHYSICIAN: I know. I mean her spirit, her image, her thought.

[*Pause.*]

THE WIFE: Did he tell you about this? [*Shakes her head disappointedly.*] What's left for us? What's left for us? He has told you this private and utterly personal secret of mine! When did he tell you? When exactly did he tell you this?

THE PHYSICIAN: Just today.

THE WIFE: Today? How . . . but . . .?

THE PHYSICIAN: He called me.

THE WIFE: Oh, the phone. I forgot to disconnect it. [*Pause.*] Why did he have to say this? How could he? Was it easy for him?

THE PHYSICIAN: Well, he said it almost with concern.

THE WIFE: Concern?! Disloyalty these days has all kinds of names, including "concern."

THE PHYSICIAN: What are you talking about? It was necessary for me to know this. If he hadn't told me, you should have. I'm your close friend and family doctor. Sooner or later you need to trust someone. In fact, if you had told me earlier, perhaps it would've not gone so far.

THE WIFE [*angry*]: You talk as if I had a dangerous disease and had been hiding it. Well, people talk to themselves. When they pray, for example, they whisper to their God. In a *saqqa-khuneh*[20] they open their hearts to candle lights; they converse with Hafez when consulting his *divan*.[21] I open my heart to my mother's spirit every now and then. What's wrong with that?

THE PHYSICIAN: I didn't say there was anything wrong. . . .

THE WIFE: One of the most important literary creations of mankind, the most important drama ever written is *Hamlet*. Hamlet talks to his father's ghost at the beginning of the play. That conversation is the key to a secret that he alone can solve. His tragic love and life are both related to this dialogue, a dialogue with a ghost.

THE PHYSICIAN: Calm down, my dear. I didn't say there's anything wrong with you. Talking with the spirit of your mother in itself is no problem; it's not even a disease. But it may be the beginning of your intentionally confusing imagination with reality, to the point that having been subjectively convinced that your husband has lost all his morality and humanity, you actually see him as a human-animal.

THE WIFE: And, of course, between the two of us—he having lost his humanity and I simply seeing the reality—it is I who has to be cured?!

THE PHYSICIAN: But the point is what you see is not reality as we commonly understand it. You have an absolute personal definition of reality, and that's the only thing you understand. Unfortunately, that definition begins with you and ends with you, and nobody else shares it with you. You talk about Hamlet; I mention a city whose people have turned into rhinoceroses; somebody else refers to ancient statues of humans with eagle or horse heads or animals with human heads. These things all come true in the vast domains of our sleep, our dreams, in man's imagination and his artistic creations, but not in the limited confines of daily life. Now within these boundaries we have to have mutually acceptable definitions of reality in order to understand each other. And such mutually acceptable definitions should be founded either on moral and legal agreements or on scientific bases. Unfortunately, science has not yet given any definition of a man with an animal's head.

THE WIFE: What about its possibility?

THE PHYSICIAN: None at all.

THE WIFE: So I have to go to a sanitarium.

THE PHYSICIAN: Well, you don't have to.

THE WIFE: How can I avoid it?

THE PHYSICIAN: Go home and see your husband as you used to.

THE WIFE: But if I go back and see that he's still an ass, then what do I do?

THE PHYSICIAN: You two must come up with an agreement: either you go to a sanitarium or he goes to a stable.

THE WIFE: But what if you were to come to our house and see him as I do?

THE PHYSICIAN: You mean an ass from the neck up?

THE WIFE: Yes.

THE PHYSICIAN: Then the two of us would have to decide which sanitarium to go to.

[*Curtain.*]

Act II
Scene Five

An autumn sunset, the crows are crowing. THE WIFE is sitting on a bench in a park. After a while the sound of footsteps of someone approaching is heard; THE WRITER appears. He looks like a tourist, with a camera hanging over his shoulder. He rushes to see THE WIFE; but once near her, he slows down.

THE WRITER: Hi!

[*THE WIFE stands up. THE WRITER wants to embrace her; but the crows scream and he changes his mind, looking around suspiciously.*[22]]

How are you? I can't believe it! When I heard you over the phone, I couldn't believe it!

THE WIFE: Why? What's so strange about that? Nobody's herself these days anyway.

THE WRITER: No, I'm serious. I was wondering if, after so many years, it were actually possible you'd call me or even remember me. It was really amazing; funny how nervous I was. Then I really pitied myself when I hung up. "You see, you wretched soul," I told myself, "your only happiness is whether she can remember you or not, let alone her calling you and asking to see you...!"

[*THE WIFE suddenly stands up and looks at the man.*]

THE WIFE: Am I ugly?

THE WRITER: What?

THE WIFE: Have I become really ugly?

THE WRITER: What are you talking about?

THE WIFE: Very, very ugly?

THE WRITER [*wants to embrace her, but the crows scream and he holds back*]: You should never ask me such a question. I am the last person on earth capable of answering that question. For me, you are light, pure light. How can I see you as ugly, even if you were?

THE WIFE: But tell me! Am I ugly or not?

THE WRITER: No, no, no! You're more beautiful than ever. Perhaps you've never been as beautiful as you are now.

THE WIFE: And do you still love me?

THE WRITER: More than ever.

THE WIFE: But isn't that just a phrase, an empty phrase, beautiful and poetic as it may be?

THE WRITER: What do you mean?

THE WIFE: I mean, is it possible to rely on words? Can one really count on them?

THE WRITER: Well, try me. I'm honest. But if I can't split my head with an ax like Farhad[23] or drink poison like Romeo, it's because I'm an ordinary man. The love of an ordinary man is just ordinary, like him.

THE WIFE: Then can I ask you an ordinary favor? Will you do it if you could?

THE WRITER: If I could; try me!

THE WIFE: Help me get out of here. I don't care how; just help me get out of here.

THE WRITER: Do you want to leave? When?

THE WIFE: As soon as possible. If you were a sorcerer or I had wings, right now.

[*The man laughs nervously.*]

I know it's difficult; but it's being done every day. I thought with the connections that you have, perhaps. . . .

THE WRITER: Have you been separated from your husband?

THE WIFE: Not yet.

THE WRITER: Do you want to be separated?

THE WIFE: Leaving is separation, isn't it?

THE WRITER: Can I ask you why?

THE WIFE: Have you ever had an unusual experience—in your imagination, perhaps—that you can't tell others because you fear their reactions?

THE WRITER: I understand. Okay, give me a few days. Let me see what I can do.

THE WIFE: A few days?

THE WRITER: It's not so easy. It may take weeks or even months.

THE WIFE: That's too late. Forget it.

THE WRITER: I'll try my best to do it as soon as possible, don't you worry; just tell me how I can get in touch with you. You see, this should be only between the two of us, even your husband. . . .

THE WIFE: I won't be going home anyway. I don't want to go home. You'll have to find me a hotel or somewhere like that until things have been taken care of.

THE WRITER: What do you mean you don't want to go home? What's going on? [*THE WIFE fixes a suppliant look on him.*] Okay, never mind. Let's just review exactly what it is you expect me to do. You want to leave the country. You have a husband. Because of your former position and present situation both you and your husband are under surveillance. If you are not officially under surveillance, then your relatives, whose curiosity should not be underestimated, are watching you. I want to help you to get out of the country illegally. I am married and have children. Just getting wind of my seeing you in a motel is enough to have me accused of adultery. What do I do for a living? I am a writer, or rather, a journalist. What's my disadvantage? Well, I am still writing. Many people who consider my writings the cause of their problems or who, with or without reason, have been hurt by my writings will be more than happy to see me in front of the firing squad or on the lashing bench. Well, for many reasons my plan to help you escape may be unsuccessful. Then the shit will hit the fan; and whatever it is you are running and hiding from will have to come out. For God's sake, at least tell me what I am going to be accountable for.

THE WIFE: What's the point of my telling you. It would add to the problems you just mentioned. No! I don't think love can do me any good either.

THE WRITER: What's love got to do with it?

THE WIFE: I had hoped that the love you kept talking about would alleviate the problems; but it actually intensifies them.

THE WRITER: If you don't want to believe my love, well don't. But at least you should know that nowadays nobody does such a thing for anybody, unless for altruistic reasons or for money. Now just suppose I were the most romantic, passionate lover in the world today. The problem is neither my romanticism nor my love; the problem is the modernity of this love. If this incident had happened two centuries ago and I had sacrificed my life for it, my love would have been remembered with pity and compassion. It would have found its way into romantic stories. But today it would be loathed, defiled, completely ridiculed. Well, what the hell! Who cares what they say? I can sacrifice myself for love if I want to. But remember that two other human beings will inherit the legacy of my scandalous name and reputation. They have had nothing to do with my love. Why should they pay for it for the rest of their lives? And I wouldn't gain anything from it either, except disappointment. But what can one do? Perhaps this is my lot, my destiny; and there isn't anything I can do.

[*THE WIFE pitifully takes his hand. The crows start crowing, and the man takes his hand away. THE WIFE regrets having touched him. She turns away.*]

Can I ask something? Not the same question you didn't answer. This is a different one. Can I ask it?

THE WIFE: Sure.

THE WRITER: As far as I remember, both you and your husband despised the previous regime; I mean, you criticized everything. Yet you kept doing your job. Your husband was a high-ranking official in the National Iranian Oil Company, and you ran a private school which was quite unique.

THE ASS   55

Obviously, you are equally critical of what's going on around you right now. Yet in this regime you don't work anymore. My question is why?

THE WIFE: Why what?

THE WRITER: Why don't you work anymore? Don't you think if you'd kept working, you wouldn't have to escape now?

THE WIFE: That's a good question. I mean in its own journalistic way, it's a good question. [*She takes a deep breath.*] Well, my dear, when my husband and I were born, the old regime existed. It existed because of all its power and historical reasons. My husband and I had not brought that regime to power. We grew up with it and got used to it. We even got used to its corruptions. We could not change what we disagreed with. When you have fallen into a loathsome and tumultuous sea, it's ridiculous to try to purify it or somehow make it change. The only thing you could do was not get drowned. That's how we were. We tried to stay afloat. But when it comes to a regime that is just taking root, then things are different. Now my husband and I are not children, without rights or without the intelligence to choose. Now by working or not working, we determine the growth of a monster that has just been born. Isn't it enough that we let this monster be conceived? Do we have to raise him too?

THE WRITER: The point is whether your refusal to work aborts the growth of this monster.

THE WIFE: Perhaps not. But when a house is on fire and you can't extinguish it, the least you can do is not pour more gasoline on it.

THE WRITER: It's not enough, don't you see? I think everybody should try to do something to stop the fire. If you want to extinguish the fire, then you have to stay close to it and do something. You can't do anything if you keep away from it.

THE WIFE: Well, Mr. Journalist! Are you doing something to extinguish the fire, or are you causing it to flare up more?

THE WRITER: You're right. I can't do a thing to abort the monster with that short column I have in the newspaper. But at least I remain on guard until I have the opportunity to strike.

THE WIFE: And you think they'll let you keep writing that useless column of yours? The first chance they get, they'll give it to somebody who's not indifferent to the growth of the monster. Then you'll have to pay any price just to hold on to a spot you've spent years of your time and energy creating. All of a sudden you'll discover that in order to hold on to your place, you'll have started shooting from it. Oh! But not *at* the monster—*for* the monster and at its command.

THE WRITER: Well, you are giving too much credit to this monster. The monster may be more powerful than me but not more intelligent. Sooner or later I'll find opportunities. Even if I don't find any, I'm more satisfied by doing something.

THE WIFE: You sound like my husband now.

THE WRITER: If he's reached the same conclusion, that's good.

[*Pause.*]

THE WIFE [*looks at her watch*]: It's getting late. They probably lock the gates in the evening.

THE WRITER: Well, what's the verdict? What do you want to do? Or rather, what do I have to do?

[*Pause.*]

THE WIFE: You are a writer, aren't you? Never mind whether you're a good or a bad writer. You are a writer, and you can use your imagination. Now think! A woman wakes up . . . in the morning . . . and sees that her husband . . . has become . . . from the neck up . . . an ass.

[*Pause.*]

THE WRITER: Oh! What a theme! [*He thinks.*] Wonderful! That's sensational! A woman wakes up in the morning and sees her husband from the neck up is. . . . Well, there are some precedents, but it's just fabulous. . . .

THE WIFE: Well, now, just imagine. . . . What did you say? Did you say it has precedents? How do you mean?

THE WRITER: I mean this idea is not something new . . . a man becoming an animal. Our own classical case is *Kalileh va Demneh*;[24] and a good modern example is Kafka's *Metamorphosis*, a man who turns into an insect.

But that's not important. If you really think about it, there aren't any new ideas anymore. There is nothing which hasn't been said before. The point is how to advance the idea.

THE WIFE: Hey . . ., hold your horses! What are you talking about? This is not an idea for a story. This has happened to me! That's why I'm asking your help to get out of here. This calamity has happened to me.

THE WRITER: Why do you have to talk about this so seriously? Why should there be something real behind all this? What's wrong with fantasy? Who believes, for example, that Kafka's *Metamorphosis* actually happened? The point is that it's a masterpiece, a remarkable achievement. Of course, the way you present your tale is bad either. The story may be narrated from the wife's perspective, as an interior monologue. Like right now, when you say that your husband has turned into an ass.

THE WIFE: Well, it seems you aren't that much of a human being either.

THE WRITER: I beg your pardon; I didn't mean any disrespect to Mr. . . . .

THE WIFE [*angry*]: The hell with all stories, articles, and all that nonsense! Why don't you understand? I'm telling you this has really happened to me. Do I have to repeat it?

THE WRITER [*looks around with horror*]: Okay, okay, I mean . . . you don't have to. . . .

THE WIFE: Do you want to come with me and see him with your own eyes? Then you may believe that he's an ass from the neck up? I mean he has two long ears on his forehead and an elongated jaw as well as a projected muzzle. I'm serious! Do you want to see him?

[*Pause. The man is speechless and confused.*]

What are you thinking about? Did I say anything during our conversation to indicate that I'm mentally or emotionally disturbed. . .? I mean, do I look like I'm going crazy?

THE WRITER: No, I was just. . . .

THE WIFE: Then why do you think I'm going crazy? Why are you doubting the soundness of my mind? I am telling you to come and . . . see him with your own eyes!

[*Pause. THE WIFE begins to cry.*]

THE WRITER: Look, maybe what I'm going to say sounds childish, but I hope, from the bottom of my heart, that this has really happened. Just as kids hope that the story of Superman is true so they, too, can imagine themselves flying someday. If what you say or something like it is actually true, I hope I'll be the first one to know it and see it.

THE WIFE: Then what are you waiting for? Let's go and see.

THE WRITER: I'm ready, I. . . .

THE WIFE: But I'm not ready. What if you come and see that what I say is actually true? Ha? You have to tell me, what will you do?

THE WRITER: I? Ha, ha, ha. . .! Well before anything else, I'd take a few pictures. . . . [*He points to his camera.*] You don't mind, do you?

THE WIFE: Not at all.

THE WRITER: It's enough to record what you're describing with this camera.

THE WIFE: Do you promise to help me get out of here, then?

THE WRITER: Get you out of here? I'll go with you. And I won't tell anybody anything, even my wife. We'll go from here, this very night. We can become millionaires just with these pictures. You, as a woman to whom this incident has happened, and I, as a journalist who recorded it with his camera, will become the most famous couple in the world. Or . . . even better, we'll cover his head and take him with us. Just imagine! We can make a bundle in the most famous circuses of the world. Imagine what we'll make with television shows and interviews. They'll have to stand in line. Oh, God, the money we could make . . . wow. . . . I only hope that what you say is actually true. Ha? [*He loses his enthusiasm.*] It is true? You're not pulling my leg, are you? You're not laughing at me for being naive, are you? Like a child, I'm building a fantasy, a dream castle out of nothing at all. . . . Ha?

[*Curtain.*]

Act III
Scene One

Back in the courtyard of the couple's house. It's night. THE WIFE is sitting close to the small garden next to the geraniums. Sounds of conversation and laughter can be heard from the living room. THE WIFE is looking in the direction of the voices. Then she looks back at the geraniums. The moon is shining.

THE WIFE: Oh mother! I need you so much tonight! It is a crucial moment in your daughter's life. There are moments in one's life that don't appear to carry the same significance as birth, love, marriage, or death, and yet they do. Tonight is one of those occasions for me. All the more or less significant men of my life are gathered here tonight: all the close relatives and friends of my husband's and mine. My father is here, so is my brother, and the first man who wanted to marry me, our family physician who is also a friend, and then a man who used to love me and claims he still does. They are all here. They've come to judge between us. Although they have come to talk about me, when I entered the room they all became silent. I felt I shouldn't be there. This is our destiny, mother: all the important decisions of our lives are made in absentia—birth, life, and death.

[*Pause. A door is opened and shut. THE HUSBAND comes to the courtyard. From the neck up he is still an ass.*]

THE HUSBAND: Why did you leave us alone?

THE WIFE: You're not alone. I am.

THE HUSBAND: Obviously. Then why don't you join us? So you won't be alone!?

THE WIFE [*sarcastically*]: Am I being summoned?

THE HUSBAND: Don't be so bitter. You invited all the guests. You wanted them to be here.

THE WIFE: But you called the doctor!

THE HUSBAND: I called the lawyer too, of course, after you'd seen him! But what's the difference; for better or worse they're the ones who are supposed to help us. What's the difference if I've asked them here or you? Now that they are here, let's see what they have to say.

THE WIFE: Okay, let's see what they have to say.

[*Blackout.*]

Mary Apick and Parviz Sayyad in their first performance of *The Ass*, Los Angeles, 1983.

Mary Apick in *The Ass*, Los Angeles, 1983.

Act III
Scene Two

When the couple enter the living room, its light is turned on. The family PHYSICIAN, THE LAWYER, THE FATHER, THE BROTHER, and THE WRITER are all sitting around a table. From the neck up, they are all asses. They are all staring at THE WIFE. She wants to escape from the room; but as she turns around, her HUSBAND is facing her.

THE HUSBAND: We were just talking about you. I was trying to explain our problem to these gentlemen. Of course it wasn't really necessary. You had already told them everything. What we have to do now is sit down and listen to what they have to say. Come, join us. If you have anything to say, let's hear it. If I have done anything wrong, just say it. Let them judge between us.

[*While this conversation is going on, THE HUSBAND seats THE WIFE in a chair facing the guests. He sits too.*]

THE WRITER: Well, somebody start.

THE LAWYER: Doctor?

THE PHYSICIAN: I really don't have too much to say; please let me speak later.

THE WRITER: Haj Aqa,[25] Haj Aqa should really start first, both because of his age and because he is the father.

THE FATHER [*addressing his daughter*]: Look here, dearest, let me tell you like it is: Your husband is absolutely right. The rest is up to you. The gentlemen who are present here already know quite well that I am not particularly fond of him. But I have to say that if he has done one thing right in his entire life, it's going back to his job. What do you expect him to do, poor soul? Get depressed and stay home with you? A woman is supposed to stay home and be a good housewife. But not a man. That's all there is to it.

THE LAWYER: With all due respect, I disagree with the last part of what Haj Aqa said. I would say if you go back to work too, it would be helpful in resolving this problem. For a woman who has always been actively engaged in a positive social function, returning to the role of a housewife with no sense of duty would have certain side effects, one of which we are now witnessing. Isn't that so, Doctor?

THE PHYSICIAN: Oh! Yes, yes, of course.

THE WRITER: You shouldn't have left your school. School is an important battle-front, I. . . .

THE LAWYER [taps on THE WRITER's shoulder]: I beg your pardon, but I'm not finished yet.

THE WRITER: Oh, I'm sorry. Please go ahead.

THE LAWYER: Thank you! [Addresses THE WIFE.] In your absence, I also made another suggestion. Take a short period of time, say, six months, as a grace period. During this period, both of you should try to immerse yourselves in your respective jobs. Then see what happens. If getting back to your jobs changes what has happened, well, so much the better. We'll get back together here and celebrate. Haj Aqa will have to promise to indulge himself on that night and have a drink with us!

THE WRITER: That's what he is doing now every night!

[THE LAWYER, THE PHYSICIAN, and THE WRITER laugh.]

THE LAWYER: But if things don't change, or if they get worse, we'll get together again and seriously consider the possibilities of divorce.

THE FATHER: I seek God's forgiveness!

THE LAWYER: Please, we have to set aside our prejudices. If things don't work out, we'll have to rely on divorce as a logical and practical solution. Especially the husband should promise right now to be cooperative. I don't have anything else to say.

THE WRITER: Before I express my personal opinion, I would like to repeat what I said before: Go back to your school. Don't leave the battle front. I know there are many problems at school. They're changing the curriculum, and you disagree with them. Well, I disagree too, but what can we do? It's better by far if a non-believer rather than a committed believer teaches that nonsense to the poor kids. Don't you see? This is the advantage of not leaving the battle front. When you are involved, you

THE ASS

feel you are doing something, not for the monster, for the kids. Now, as for my own personal opinion [*points to his camera*], I wish the pictures of that imaginative and beautiful creature who could open the gates of fame and fortune to us were registered here. But we can still work on it, if you agree we can do something with it as a joint project. Perhaps if school doesn't satisfy you, this will. Think about it; I am always ready.

THE PHYSICIAN: As a physician, I recommend resting rather than activity at this time. Perhaps there is a difference of opinion among us as to whether women should work or not. But I don't think anybody would disagree with my suggestion about the necessity of rest.

THE FATHER: Why don't you go to your aunt's at the Caspian Sea? Go and stay with her for a while. Come back when you feel better.

THE PHYSICIAN: If you don't feel particularly resentful of the name "asylum," that would be my first suggestion. Otherwise, I would recommend a trip to a small town or village far from the hustle and bustle of the city. You can always resume your activities if you are physically and mentally healthy. Priority should now be given to your health, which is more important than anything else.

[*Pause. THE WIFE looks at her BROTHER, who is sitting in a corner, away from the others. Under the weight of her look, he begins to speak.*]

THE BROTHER: Well, do as they say. The life you've chosen for yourself has its own problems, as well as solutions. You've been afflicted by its problems, and its solutions are what they suggest. You don't have any other choice. Either do what they tell you, or else commit suicide. They are both equally acceptable to me.

[*Pause. THE HUSBAND comes near his WIFE; puts his hand over her shoulder.*]

THE HUSBAND: Don't you want to offer our guests some tea?

[*THE WIFE calmly stands up and leaves the room.*]

THE WRITER: Is there another beverage here other than tea?

THE PHYSICIAN: Let's have the tea first.

THE LAWYER: Have you heard the one about the guy they wanted to whip because he had drunk some wine?

THE WRITER: Which one? It has many versions.

THE LAWYER: A drunken fellow was taken to a *komiteh*[26] to be whipped. The head of the *komiteh* asked him, "You got drunk again?" He said, "Yessir!" The man asked, "Didn't you know you'll get a hundred lashes on your ass?" "Yessir!" he answered. "How dare you get drunk again?" "Well, sir," he said, "I have my ass's permission, sir!"

[*They all laugh. The telephone rings. THE HUSBAND wants to pick up the phone. THE BROTHER prevents him.*]

THE BROTHER: No phone calls while I am here. Don't answer it! You promised.

THE HUSBAND: Okay, I forgot. I apologize.

[*The phone rings a number of times.
Blackout.*]

Act III
Scene Three

THE WIFE comes to the courtyard. She has a suitcase in her hand and is dressed to go out. She sits down near the small garden.

THE WIFE: They have asked me to leave, mother; [*Pause*] and I'm leaving. Where to, I don't know. But not where they want me to go. [*Long pause.*] From the day of creation, there have always been two major questions: Why is one born, and why should one die? I think the second question is superfluous. There is only one question: Why do we come to this world? Why? [*Pause.*] I have had a better life than you did, mother. That's why I don't blame you for bringing me into this world. But I will never forgive my grandmother for giving birth to you.

[*She wipes away her tears. THE HUSBAND comes to the courtyard. THE WIFE gets up to leave.*]

THE HUSBAND: What are you doing here? Are you going somewhere? Where? [*Pause.*] Who are you escaping from? Me? Or yourself?

[*THE WIFE motions to leave. THE HUSBAND prevents her.*]

Wait a minute. At least hear me out before you go. Our friends have told us what they had to say. But I haven't said anything yet. Now that you are leaving me, at least hear me out. Sit down here, right here. You've put up with me for so long, a few more minutes shouldn't be too much trouble.

[*He takes the suitcase and puts it near the garden. Then he makes her sit on the suitcase.*]

You can accuse me of whatever you want, but don't deny me the right to defend myself; or at least the right of a final plea. Hear me out, and then if you want, or if you can, you may go. [*Pause.*] Well, what can I say? Where can I begin? Oh, yes, in that room our friends—whose friendship, by the way, is not without animosity either—all sided with me, despite all you had done today to convince them otherwise. They came to the same conclusion that I had. But now let me tell you something else, dearest. What they say is logical. That's right, it's logical. But it's not right. *You* are right. What *you* see is true. I have turned into an ass. Yes, I admit it, I am an ass. But what's wrong with that? You see, everybody is a little bit of an ass anyway! I may be more of an ass than others. Well, so be it. What's wrong with an ass? It's an ass, the poor thing! It's not a sin to be an ass. No, wait a minute, let me finish. I know what you want to say. No, I am not being facetious. I mean, like a person who is drowning I may try to reach for something, anything, to hold on to. I know, I'm not consistent; but neither are you. Why didn't anybody believe you? Ha, I ask you, why? Because you didn't make sense to them. But I believe you, because you speak with the language of your heart, and I know your heart. What I'm telling you now is also not logical or believable. It may not be believable even to you who knows my heart; but it's at least worth listening to because it's my heart's word. [*Pause.*] Yes, I was talking about the animal, about the good qualities of the ass. Believe me, the ass really isn't a bad human being . . . sorry, I mean a bad animal. He's patient, tolerant, hardworking, content, and thankful. Believe me, even the stubborn ones are quite beneficial. You see, an ass is a helpful beast; it's not constantly nagging and bitching. He goes on about his own business, doing his job patiently. Oh! How man would brag and congratulate himself, if only he had some of these qualities! But the ass, the poor thing, it's as if he's born to be good, to be helpful, and not even keep his nose up or be a pompous ass for being so good and helpful. [*Pause.*] I don't know why and based on what justification this poor creature is accused of stupidity. It is a totally baseless and unjust accusation that only man is capable of making. Who says the ass is stupid? In comparison to what animal is he stupid? You load him up a number of times and take him somewhere, and he finds his way back to the stable; you don't have to guide him anymore. Gracefully and calmly he finds his way home. And on his way home, he doesn't bother a soul; he doesn't pick anybody's pocket or push somebody around. He never whores around; he doesn't abuse people with four-letter words either. And then, in the face of all this nobility, reverence, and respect we say: "O leave him alone; he's just a stupid ass!" Those who call the ass stupid should really consider their own behavior! They whip the poor creature, stick all kinds of needles and what-not into him just because he won't pass quickly over a cliff, for example, or because he slows down when he approaches a stinking ditch in the ground, or because he refuses to jump over a wide creek. Well now, really? Who is stupid here? He who sees the danger and proceeds cautiously or that heartless tyrant who rains blows on the poor creature's behind until he bleeds just because he's cautious? Man indulges himself in being conservative in his own affairs a hundred times more than he tolerates precautions from the ass. He tortures the poor animal; and after all, the ass is only being cautious for his master's sake. . . . [*Pause.*] What really burns me up is accusing the

THE ASS

ass of thoughtlessness. They say the ass never thinks. Who says the ass never thinks!? The ass is the greatest living thinker in the world! You laugh? You think I'm not making sense, ha? You think I'm just joking? But of course an ass thinks and thinks much deeper than man, who is so sure of his intelligence. Well, suppose his thinking doesn't get him anywhere? If he can't come to a conclusion, that doesn't mean he isn't thinking. Anyone who carefully watches an ass for a while will come to the same conclusion—there isn't a more thoughtful creature in the world. This really doesn't need any laboratory research or anything like that. This is simply verifiable through observation. You just tie an ass to a tree in a prairie or, forget about that, just tie him to a parking meter in a street, stand aside, and watch him. It's exactly as if you'd parked your car; he'll just stay there without moving. What do you think he's doing there other than thinking? You see that he's not asleep; he moves his eyelids. But he's totally indifferent to his surroundings. Nothing distracts him; nothing causes him any astonishment. Why? Because he's thinking. With complete concentration and total mobilization of his mental faculties, he's thinking. Now, if all of a sudden you make a noise, say, blow a horn or something, he'll jump. You've just distracted him from deep thought. It's even possible that he'll make some nervous move, like a person who's just been suddenly awakened from a dream by a horrifying sound. He may just stampede and go wild. I realize he rarely comes to any conclusion through his thinking; but that's not his fault. The poor thing tries his best, but he falls short of any conclusion that would allow him to be effectively creative, as we say nowadays, and change his life for the better. Well, it's really nature's fault, not his, that he doesn't have enough mental energy and brain cells. The poor animal is really in pain because of this. It's quite obvious; look at his face. [*THE WIFE laughs quietly.*] No! This is really not funny. This is tragic. If you see a poor kid who studies day in and day out and yet fails in his exams as a result of some defect in his mental abilities, would you laugh or feel sorry? Well, it's really pitiful. [*Pause.*] I have asked myself a number of times, what does that ass really think about? It's quite clear from his face that he's constantly searching for an answer to a question. He's caught in a "Why." A "Why." It's as if he is asking "Why?" Why what, I really don't know. But doesn't everything—and I mean the whole universe, creation, existence, nature, the incredible movement of the planets, the amazing destiny of man—I mean doesn't everything fall into a big question mark? In a big "Why"? Don't you think that the ass's complete obliviousness to his surroundings and the fact that nothing amazes him, that nothing makes him quite happy or really sad, is an indication of his absolute preoccupation with a deep philosophical question? Don't you think, for example, that the ass asks himself, "To be or not to be?"[27] Where did Hamlet end up in trying to find an answer to this question? He reached his own annihilation. What have we come to? Our civilization is the end-result of centuries of thinking. But is this civilization worth the heavy price we have paid for it? With all these modern luxuries—refrigerators, televisions, electricity, highways, airplanes, and so forth—are we as content as an ass? When we really think about it, we see there is almost no solution to this problem. Then, since we don't have the patience and perseverance of the ass, we quit, and we don't think about it anymore. But the poor ass who is caught in the trap of perpetual deliberation follows this futile thinking persistently from the day he reaches maturity until his last day. It's as if he's damned eternally. The eternal damnation of thinking, not coming to any conclusion, and yet not giving up. That's the bitter essence of tragedy. What do you think the myth of Sisyphus is all about? In their anger and wrath, the gods had condemned Sisyphus to carry a huge rock to the summit of a mountain on his bare shoulders. But each time he reached the summit, the rock rolled back down to the foot of the mountain, and Sisyphus had to retrieve it and carry it back up to the summit again. This went on until the end of time. If the tragedy of Sisyphus is something of a myth, the tragedy of our poor animal, the ass, is absolute reality. Every ass is the objective expression of the tragedy of Sisyphus. Now multiply this by the number of asses in the world, generation after generation. [*Pause.*] The biggest advantage of the ass is his self-understanding, you know, his knowledge of who he really is. An ass is totally aware of his advantages and disadvantages, his abilities and disabilities. He knows what he's capable of and what he is not. Have you ever seen an ass composing poetry? Especially composing bad poetry and trying to make it pass for good poetry? Have you ever seen an ass being pretentious about his erudition? Or constantly criticizing everything, and taking issue with everyone, and then even calling himself a critic? He would never do anything of the sort, because he knows his abilities as well as his limitations. Let me give you a better example. The ass really has a bad voice. Everybody knows this, even the ass himself. And because he knows he has a bad voice, he tries his best to stay quiet. Have you ever heard an ass sing? One rarely hears his voice. The fact that every once in a while he heehaws has a logic to it. No, I'm serious. Every once in a while he heehaws so that he won't forget that he has a voice. He occasionally brays as if to tell people, "Do you hear my heehaw? That's my voice! I can drive you to insomnia with this voice. I can torture you and make your life miserable. But despite all the injustices and tyrannies that you have perpetrated on me, I won't use my weapon against you. Because I have a noble character. I am more noble and forgiving than you." Yes, that's the ass, the symbol of virtue and piety. That's all right, go ahead and laugh. Make fun of me! I'll prove it to you. Read all the history books about man and other animals. Show me an instance where an ass has started a war, told a lie, committed treason or murder. Show me one instance of his having appropriated somebody else's rights, or fooled people by false promises of worldly and heavenly rewards, or mobilized a crowd behind himself out of sheer ambition, or fancied leadership, kingship, power, government, or claimed religious authority, or falsely accused somebody, or passed a wrong judgment. You show me one such instance, and I will abandon this new position of asshood to which I have just been elevated. You do that, and I will repent and resume my human shape. [*Pause.*] The only problem with the ass is—and I think this is what's bothering you—that he never complains. Well, why should he? What can he change with his complaint? Don't you know the ass himself is constantly trying to decide whether to complain or not? You think he doesn't know that if he just threw this load away and kicked and capered around—which he occasionally does, by the way, when he can't take it anymore—he won't get anywhere; he'll only increase his pain, suffering, and torture? I mean, really, why complain? "Since the chamberlain cuts everyone with the sword. . .?"[28] Among God's angels only one disobeyed; they called him Iblis and threw him out of the Divine presence and condemned him to eternal damnation. I mean, truly, don't you think that the ass's relationship to man is reminiscent of the absolute obedience of the angels to God? And so, shouldn't I be proud that I'm an ass and not a dictator?

At any rate, something that hasn't been paid attention to, or, if so, it hasn't been enough, is our failure to realize and demonstrate the ass's beauty. This negligence should really be attributed to poets, writers, and artists. Of course, I am not trying to praise myself, because I may incidentally be a rather ugly ass. But generally speaking, and as it pertains to his essence, the ass is beautiful. Some consider peacocks or chicks or kittens beautiful. Others think birds or fish are beautiful. But I believe the most beautiful living creature in this world is a baby ass. That's right. Have you ever looked at a foal? It's impossible to look at a baby ass and not have a deep urge to hug him and kiss him. Show a foal to the most obnoxious person in the world, and a smile will appear on his face. You may say monkeys are cute, too. Well, that's right; but that's because monkeys are ridiculous. Being ridiculous is different from being beautiful. Monkeys are ridiculous; baby asses are beautiful. Monkeys are shrewd; baby asses are innocent. These are two different things. As for me, I'm really sorry I became a grown ass and didn't remain a baby ass. [*Pause.*] Now, seriously, do you really want to leave me? [*Pause.*] Today, when you locked me in and left, I started thinking, like an ass tied to a parking meter. I wondered: "Why do I hurt this woman so much? She's right, you see; I am an ass. Why should I be ashamed of being an ass? Why should

I deny that I am an ass? I should really, in all honesty, accept that I look more like an ass than a human being. And that's good because as a human being I'm sinful; but as an ass, innocent. My being a human has to do with appearances and deception, while my being an ass, fortunately, involves truth and meaning. It's true that I'm an ass; and as much as I'm an ass, I am also innocent." Now you really want to leave me just because I'm an ass? Well, what's wrong with that? Perhaps this is my limit and I can go no further. Why do you want to raise me to your own level? Perhaps I don't have in me what it takes to be you. Your mind's eye is open now. You see things that are closed to most others. I'm like the others. This strange sensitivity of yours is not accorded to everybody. I'm just like others. The nature of the desert cannot give life to anything but dry bushes and thorns. Now, what can I do if you've grown like a wild flower in the middle of the desert? I'm nothing but twig and thorn. You are an exception; I am the rule. You are Hallaj,[29] you are Hafez, you are Nima,[30] you are God Himself. I'm just an ordinary man. Being ordinary is not a sin, you see; I can't do anything about that. You and I started together. We both intended to advance beyond our ordinary limitations. Well, you succeeded. I didn't. But I don't know how. I really don't know how you surpassed your boundaries and ascended so high. I just don't know. I remained behind. I fell short of catching up with you. I lost my energy. I was caught in earthly fetters and could not fly with you. But now that you've reached that height and I'm left behind in this muddy and stinking pit, do you really want to leave me? Is this your sense of fidelity? Moreover, where will you go? What if you left and you saw everybody was just like me? In the street, in the city, overseas, if everywhere you saw people were just like me, what would you do? What really bothers me about your leaving is not that I will be alone. We asses are absolutely in the majority. But you will be alone, I mean deadly alone. [*Pause.*] I didn't seek you hand in marriage through conventional ways; we didn't get to know each other in high school or at a party. We came together through love; we knew each other by love; we sat together under the shade of love, in the fresh air of love. [*Pause.*] Now why do you want to leave me? Just because I can't reach you? Would you have left me if I were infected by the plague? Or if I were handicapped? So what if I've become an ass? [*Pause.*] Stay with me. [*Pause.*] For God's sake, what else can I say?! What more can I say?! What more do you want?! I accept that I'm an ass! An ass! An ass! But I love you. Despite all my asininity, I love you. Try to understand me. Try to understand my asininity. Don't leave me. I'll be a desperate ass without you, a sick ass, a wretched ass.

THE ASS

[*He puts his head down and begins to cry. THE WIFE stands up. She kneels next to her HUSBAND and caresses him.*]

THE WIFE: Okay. Come on now, that's enough.

[*THE HUSBAND mumbles something while crying.*]

I said it's enough now. It's not good for our guests to see you like this.

THE HUSBAND: Will you stay?

THE WIFE: Yes, you win. I'll stay.

THE HUSBAND [*laughing*]: Oh! My dearest!

[*They embrace each other.*]

THE WIFE: My husband, my father, my brother, my friend, my love, my donkey, I love you.

[*THE HUSBAND laughs heartily.*]

What are you doing, you silly?! The neighbors will hear you. [*She starts to groom her HUSBAND.*] Now tell me, you devil, did you come up with all this just today while I kept you locked in?

THE HUSBAND: Oh! What can I tell you, if someday the poor asses of the world could talk. . . .

THE WIFE: Okay. Please don't start all over again. Maybe some other time. I must take some tea to our guests. They've been so nice; they haven't said anything so far.

[*THE WIFE goes into the building.*]

THE HUSBAND [*to himself*]: That's good to know! She already thinks it's nice not to complain! So far, so good! So far, so good!

[*Blackout.*]

Act III
Scene Four

The light is on in the living room. The guests are conversing and laughing.

THE WRITER: Have you heard the one about Akbari and Asqari?

THE PHYSICIAN: No, which one?

THE WRITER: Well, Haj Aqa may get offended.

THE LAWYER: That's alright; he'll laugh. If it's funny, he'll laugh; don't worry about it.

THE WRITER: Well. This passion for martyrdom was really getting into Akbari and Asqari; and they were just full of it. They both decided to go to the war and get themselves martyred. Akbari gets his wish quickly. As soon as he gets to the front, he walks on a mine and gets his ass blown up and goes right to paradise. But the poor Asqari isn't as lucky. He's injured, taken to a hospital, and one of his legs is amputated. Now, he was really down. Akbari got himself martyred and was now enjoying himself in paradise, while he was left amputated on a hospital bed.

[*THE WIFE enters with a tray full of tea-cups. She is now also an ass from the neck up. All present burst into applause.*]

THE FATHER: Well, it's about time we finally got a lousy cup of tea.

THE PHYSICIAN: About time, indeed.

THE WIFE: Sorry I'm late. My husband was explaining something. . . .

THE LAWYER: So what happened next?

THE WRITER: Well, I'll tell you later.

THE WIFE: What is it? Are you telling "dirty jokes"?[31]

THE WRITER: Just a little bit dirty.

THE WIFE: That's alright. If it's just a little bit, please go on.

THE PHYSICIAN: Come on now! Let's hear it!

THE WRITER: At any rate, Asqari was really dying of envy that Akbari had been killed and gone to paradise and was now enjoying himself. Finally, he sees Akbari one night in his dream. Lo and behold, Akbari is lying on a beautiful silk bed. Behind him is a gorgeous panorama of paradise; and he has a carafe of wine in one hand and a beautiful girl in the other. Asqari says: "You son-of-a-bitch Akbari, you call yourself a friend? You left me all alone in this world while you enjoy yourself there in paradise? Weren't we supposed to become martyrs together?" Akbari says: "Asqari, dear friend, don't get upset. Believe me, you are much better off than me." Asqari bombarded Akbari with every obscenity he could think of. "You ought to be ashamed of yourself," he exploded, "you asshole. You have a golden carafe of wine in one hand and that gorgeous thing—Oh God, what a beauty—in the other; and here in this hospital if you die, they won't give you a drop of booze and all the nurses are male, and if every once in a while you find a female nurse, she has a mustache, for God's sake. Sons of bitches, I don't know where in the world they find female nurses with mustaches. And you say I'm better off than you?" Akbari complained: "But my dear Asqari, you don't know what I'm going through here in this so-called paradise. What can I tell you? Now look! This carafe of wine you see here has a huge hole. They pour wine in it; but as soon as I try to drink it, the goddamn stuff just spills out. But to make matters worse, look at this beautiful thing lying next to me. The bitch doesn't have a hole in her entire body."

[*Laughter, confusion, and coughing of all present. Blackout.*]

Act III
Scene Five

In the courtyard the small garden is lit. THE HUSBAND, who has been looking into the living room from there, pauses for a while. Then he takes the mask of the ass off. He turns around and looks at the geranium.

THE HUSBAND: Can you hear me? [*Looks at the empty space.*] Huh? Do you hear me, mother? [*Pause.*] I wish you could hear me. I wish there were somebody who could hear me.

[*Curtain.*]

The Ass was first performed on May 13, 1983, at the Assistant League Playhouse in Los Angeles with the following cast:

Mary Apik:	THE WIFE
Parviz Sayyad:	THE HUSBAND THE BROTHER THE FATHER THE LAWYER THE PHYSICIAN THE WRITER
Other Assistants:	M. Marzban, A. Abkar, S. Khavari, R. Zakeri, A. Sharif
Sound:	Y. Shahab J. Eshrati
Setting:	A. Farrokh-Tehrani S. Bazleh
Light:	V. Noorbakhsh
Technical Assistant:	S. Khavari
Masks:	H. Baghdasarian E. Kucharian
Producer and Director:	Parviz Sayyad

NOTES

1. In the original Persian, THE HUSBAND's use of "us" and "we" in referring to himself in Persian indicates a certain pompous loftiness.
2. The sudden change in THE HUSBAND's tone, from presumptuous loftiness to perfunctory humility, is a symptom of his wife's pronouncement that he has turned into an ass.
3. The reference here is to a French movie, *Les Diaboliques* (1954), directed by Henri-George Clousot: A sadistic headmaster's wife and mistress conspire to murder him; but his body disappears and evidence of his presence haunts them. The screenplay was based on Pierre Boileau and Thomas Narcejac's *The Woman Who Was*. (For a synopsis, see Leslie Halliwell, *Halliwell's Film Guide*, 4th ed. [New York: Charles Scribner's Sons, 1977], s.v. *Les Diaboliques*.)
4. THE BROTHER is actually THE WIFE's stepbrother, the son of her deceased mother's rival wife (*havou*).
5. THE BROTHER's reference here is to George Bernard Shaw and his *Man and Superman*.
6. THE WIFE's reference here is to the ritualistic body movements in a Muslim prayer.
7. In the Islamic tradition, Ibrahim intended to sacrifice Ishmael, not Isaac.
8. Qur'an, II: 156.
9. Paraphrase of this verse of the Persian poet Sa'di (d. 1291) in *Golestan*:
   They preach to people to denounce the World;
   But they make their own bundle of silver and gold.
(M. A. Foroughi, ed., *Koliyyat-e Sa'di* [Tehran: Amir Kabir, 1363/1984], p. 92.)
10. "Hypocrite" (*al-munafiq*, pl. *al-munafiqun*), a Qur'anic term (VIII: 49; IX: 64, etc.) resuscitated by the Islamic Republic for the enemies of the state, particularly applied to members of the *Mojahedin-e Khalq* guerilla organization.
11. Alcoholic beverages have been banned by the Islamic Republic. Offering them to one's guests is a sign of defiance against the state. Refusing to offer them, as here in the case of THE LAWYER, is an indication of prudent conservatism and thus a tacit approval of the regime.
12. "What can I do for you?" The phrase in the original text is in English.
13. Hafez (d. 1389), considered to be the greatest Persian lyric poet.
14. The reference here is to Friedrich Durrenmat's *Hercules und der Stall des Augias* (Zurich, 1963). This play was staged in Iran by Hamid Samandarian. Incidentally, Parviz Sayyad played the character referred to in the text.
15. The explanation in note 10 is not applicable to this usage of "hypocrite." Here THE WIFE uses the word in an ordinary way, obviously having no specific religious connotations.
16. "I think this is a line from the movie *Ragbar (Downpour)*." Note by Parviz Sayyad. (*Ragbar* [1971], directed by Bahram Beiz'i, was a critically acclaimed motion picture—H.D.)
17. The reference is to "the Islamization" programs of the public education system by the Islamic Republic, in which, for example, the names in reading texts have been changed from "Azar," which is a pre-Islamic Iranian name, to "Zobeideh," which is Arabic/Islamic.
18. *Tarikh-e Beyhaqi*, the monumental history of Abu al-Fadl Muhammad b. Husayn Kateb (Dabir) Beyhaqi, the Persian historian and statesman of the eleventh century (995-1077). The *Annals*, according to Beyhaqi himself, commence with the year 1018. But a large portion of the work has been lost. The entire *Annals* is said to have been thirty volumes. For a critical edition, see A. A. Fayyaz, ed., *Tarikh-e Beyhaqi* (Mashhad: Ferdowsi University Press, 1356/1977).

19. A Persian (stringed) instrument.

20. *Saqqa khuneh*: a small shrine, usually an enclosed cubicle in which candles are lit and water is served to the visitors. In providing water, the shrine is particularly commemorative of the third Shi'ite Imam, Huseyn, who was martyred (680), along with his companions while, according to popular belief, thirsty.

21. The ghazals of Hafez are consulted regularly as a source of guidance and inspiration. The ritual through which this is done involves whispering one's wishes into the Divan and then asking Hafez for his guidance.

22. In the Iranian folk mythologies, the crow is an informer.

23. Farhad is the hero of the classical Persian romance, *Khosrow and Shirin*, composed by Nizami Ganjavi (1140-1203), as the second component of his quintet (*Khamsah*). The other four parts are *Makhzan al-asrar, Leyla and Majnun, Alexander the Great*, and *Haft Peykar*. *Khosrow and Shirin* is a romance of central significance in Persian literature. Having received the false news of his beloved Shirin's death, Farhad kills himself by splitting his head open with the ax he had used to cut through the Bisutun mountain, a task for which he was supposed to receive Shirin's hand. The false news had been dispatched to Farhad by his rival for Shirin's love, Khosrow.

24. *Kalileh va Demneh*: Of Indian origin, first translated into Pahlavi during the reign of King Khosrow Anushiravan (ruled 531-579 A.D.). From Pahlavi it was rendered into Syriac, Arabic, and other languages. The Arabic version, by Ibn al-Mugaffa', became the source of all but one subsequent translation (the Tibetan rendition was directly from the Sanskrit). Its Persian translation by Abu al-Ma'ali Nasru'llah b. Muhammad b. Abd al-Hamid is one of the most significant sources of the classical Persian literature. A paramount example of didactic literature, *Kalileh va Demneh* relates ethical principles through stories whose chief characters are animals. The reference of THE WRITER to this text as an antecedent of a metamorphosis is actually erroneous. In *Kalileh va Demneh* men have not turned into animals; but, conversely, animals assume human characteristics.

25. Haj Aqa: a polite and reverential form of addressing men known for their religious piety. It indicates that they have performed their pilgrimage to Mecca. THE WRITER has a certain air of sarcasm to his tone.

26. *Komiteh*. Local militia centers; *de facto* police stations. From the English "committee."

27. "To be or not to be." In the original text, this phrase is in English.

28. A hemistich in a ghazal of Hafez. The complete line is:
Since the chamberlain cuts everyone with the sword,
No one shall remain secure in the sanctuary.

29. Mansur al-Hallaj (858-922), Persian mystic, martyred in Baghdad because of esoteric pronouncements, symbolized in his famous statement: *Ana al-Haqq* (*I Am the Truth*).

30. Nima Yushij (1895-1959), the founding father of the modernist Persian poetry.

31. In the original, "dirty jokes" is in English.

Parviz Sayyad

The Rex Cinema Trial

A Play in Three Acts

Translated from the Persian with Annotations by

M. R. Ghanoonparvar

Watching the rehearsal of *The Rex Cinema Trial* first performed in Los Angeles in 1987.

THE REX CINEMA TRIAL

Characters:

MAS'UD TALA'I (the DIRECTOR)

HOSEYN TAKBE'ALIZADEH

ALISHAHI (the PROSECUTOR)

JA'FARI-TABRIZI (the JUDGE)

LIEUTENANT BAHMANI

GOVERNMENT EMPLOYEE

OWNER OF THE THEATER

COLONEL

MANAGER OF THE THEATER

GUARDS

Preparing for the performance of *The Rex Cinema Trial* in Washington, DC.

Act I
Scene One

The curtain is drawn. The auditorium and stage represent the Taj Cinema in Abadan, which has been designated as the courtroom where a trial is to be held.[1] *Mas'ud Tala'i (the DIRECTOR) walks around the auditorium for a few minutes. As though no one else were in the theater, he whistles a tune and looks around at the ceiling, the lights, and the seats. When he reaches the front of the stage, he begins to talk to himself and to the projection booth.*

DIRECTOR: Taj Cinema in Abadan. The city of the oil industry. A theater that used to show a new movie in English every few nights for the high-ranking employees and their wives. But who could have thought that such a theater would now become the scene of a historical trial? And who could have thought that I, Mas'ud Tala'i, movie director, producer of "Gavazn-ha," would be put in charge of filming, recording, and televising this very historical trial?[2] [*Pause.*] Hmm. And people still say that life is sweet. It is bitter; it is tragic; it is comic; I don't know, it is nonsense; it is garbage! No, my dear, it is none of these; it is a joke. Life is merely a joke. Yep. It was in '74 or '75, I don't quite remember. I was filming here somewhere. A friend who worked for the oil company had invited me to the Taj Cinema. He had gotten me a pass and we had come here. They were showing some American-made B movie. I asked the theater manager if they had ever shown an Iranian movie. "An Iranian movie?" he asked. I said, "Yes, an Iranian movie. Our movies now win prizes in all the international festivals and are getting awards right and left. I thought this was Iran and these oil company employees were all Iranians. Doesn't this oil that is helping you all make a living come out of Iranian soil?" The manager, of course, had no say in it. They had given him a set of instructions, which he followed to the letter, like a sheep. He said so himself. I wanted to ask him: if those instructions included putting some human excrement on a plate and having you eat it, would you eat it? In any case, this was how these gentlemen thought of the work of Iranians. They all had an absolute sense of being slaves to foreigners, everyone, from top to bottom. All doors were wide open for the import of foreign-made products. A bunch of snooty nouveau riches, with their noses held up in the air, were put in charge of a country. They were neither really proud of anything it had nor did they have any respect for its people. And how they went out of their way to provide all sorts of resources merely for some foreigner to come here and make a movie. We told them: These jerks have all they need; give some of these resources to the Iranian film makers—give them half of it, a third of it, a fifth, a tenth of it. But who would listen? How much could they take in in brokers' fees or bribes for a movie with a budget of 600,000 or 700,000 *tomans*? You need a deal worth several million dollars for some broker or wheeler-dealer with ties to the government and the Royal Court to be able to scrape out at least a million dollars. In short, they crapped so much on this country that you couldn't wash it up with an ocean full of soap and water. Look! Even its revolution can't accomplish anything. It has only stirred up the muck some more, and now you can smell the shit even more. They summoned my wife to Evin Prison for questioning, as if her singing were responsible for all the corruption and problems that made these people make a revolution! [*Notices that someone is trying, with difficulty, to come out from behind the curtain.*] What is it? Who's there?

Act I
Scene Two

HOSEYN TAKBE'ALIZADEH comes out from behind the curtain and stands at the front of the stage. He is carrying an inexpensive tape player like a book. He is about 22 or 23 years of age.

HOSEYN: Hello, Mr. Tala'i. They told me you were here.

DIRECTOR: Who are you?

HOSEYN: I am Hoseyn Takbe'alizadeh. [*Holds out his hand.*] Pleased to meet you.

DIRECTOR [*does not shake hands*]: What can I do for you?

HOSEYN: I want to take part in the trial.

DIRECTOR: Whatever for?

HOSEYN: I started the Rex Cinema fire. [*Pause.*]

DIRECTOR: Aren't you ashamed of yourself? You claim to have burned four hundred human beings alive, and now you walk around as if nothing has happened and then even try to shake hands with me?

HOSEYN: I'm sorry. [*Withdraws his hand.*]

DIRECTOR [*in a loud voice addressing the control room*]: Open the curtain. [*The curtain is opened. The DIRECTOR goes on the stage. There are chairs and tables scattered around with some television filming and reporting equipment. A camera stands on a tripod, along with television monitors, etc.*] Can you hear me? Two tables for the judge and the prosecutor, right here, facing each other. The place for the defendant, here, at the top of the triangle. I convinced them, contrary to what is common practice, to place the defendant a bit more elevated than the judge. . . . Simple white lighting for all three. An additional spotlight from the opposite upper corner for the defendant.

HOSEYN [*standing in the middle of the stage, not knowing what to do*]: Do you need any help?

DIRECTOR: No! Don't touch anything! [*He begins moving things around himself and mechanically talking to the control room.*] Now, tell me, did you really have a hand in this affair or are you just talking?

HOSEYN: Why would I lie, sir?

DIRECTOR: Nowadays, some people say a lot of things just to make a name for themselves.

HOSEYN: In this particular case, I wouldn't get anything but people spitting on me and cursing me.

DIRECTOR: Then why didn't you say anything before?

HOSEYN: Didn't say anything? Pooh! Nobody believes me. They say I've lost my mind. Yesterday I went to Haj Aqa Khorrami. I said, "These people are putting a group on trial; why don't you do something for me? You are a man of God." [*He laughs.*] He says, "Look, Hoseyn, people have all agreed that it was SAVAK's doing. And that was why they poured into the streets and overthrew the regime and sent it on its way. Now, anyone who hears your claim will think SAVAK has paid you to take the blame?" I saw that he was right. Wouldn't you have thought so yourself?

DIRECTOR: What?

HOSEYN: That it was SAVAK's doing.

DIRECTOR: I knew from the beginning that it was the work of the religious groups.

HOSEYN: Sure. How come you didn't say anything yourself?

DIRECTOR: It was different then. It was the expedient thing for everyone to say that it was SAVAK's doing.

HOSEYN: You see?

DIRECTOR: What do you mean, "You see?" You are a criminal, you son of a bitch. You can't compare yourself to me. They should have arrested you and cut you to pieces.

HOSEYN: They did, sir. They arrested me, both before and after the revolution.

DIRECTOR: Well, how come you got out?

HOSEYN: During the Shah's time, they sent me from Abadan to Tehran to the Royal Guards. When the revolution happened, I got out of prison along with all the rest.

DIRECTOR: And later?

HOSEYN: After the revolution, too, Mr. Sarrafi, the interrogator for the Abadan Prosecutor's Office, sent me to jail, but they got me out.

DIRECTOR: Who got you out?

HOSEYN: Haj Aqa Ja'fari.

DIRECTOR: Which Ja'fari? Hojjat al-Islam?[3] The judge presiding over this trial?

HOSEYN: Yes, sir.

DIRECTOR: Does he know you? Did he know you?

HOSEYN: Are you kidding? Haj Aqa Ja'fari knew both me and the others.

DIRECTOR: What others?

HOSEYN: The other guys involved in this.

DIRECTOR: In what?

HOSEYN: The Rex Cinema.

DIRECTOR: Who are these others?

HOSEYN: Kiavash, Abolpur, Mirsofyani, Hayat, God rest his soul, Bazrkar.... And Haj Aqa himself. We went to him for meetings at Qods Mosque with the public prayer leader.

DIRECTOR: Qods Mosque?

HOSEYN: Formerly called Farahabad . . . or at the home of Mr. Rashidian.

DIRECTOR: Wait a minute. Mohammad Rashidian, the representative of Abadan to the Parliament?

HOSEYN: That's right. Ask Haj Aqa yourself. [*Silence.*] I thought you knew what was going on.

DIRECTOR [*irritated*]: The hell you thought I knew what was going on. What do you mean, jackass, I knew what was going on?

HOSEYN: You said yourself you knew what was going on. . . . You said you knew the religious groups did it.

DIRECTOR: Not the way you think. I just guessed. Everybody guessed. Anyone with a little intelligence could figure out that a regime wanting to keep the people preoccupied at any price wouldn't risk destroying their confidence in the best and cheapest means of entertainment, which is the movies. [*The DIRECTOR moves around as he talks. He bumps into the microphone stand, knocking it over. HOSEYN bends over and puts it back.*] Don't touch it! Move out of the way!

HOSEYN: I wanted to h. . . .

DIRECTOR: I don't need help! Get off the stage! You are not allowed to touch anything!

HOSEYN: You think my hands are unclean? [*The DIRECTOR pushes him towards the stairs that lead to the auditorium.*]

DIRECTOR: I wish you were just unclean. I wish your whole body were merely covered with shit, which it is! If what you claim is true, you are the most despicable criminal in history. What do you mean, unclean? Unclean can be washed with water. Is there anything in the world that can clean the filth off your hands?

HOSEYN [*humiliated*]: Well, that is why I want to be put on trial, sir.

DIRECTOR: I can't figure it out. What do I have to do with all this? Why have they dragged me into this? [*Sits in a chair in the midst of the clutter and looks around helplessly. Long silence.*] Hmm. The instigator of the crime becomes the judge in the trial for the same crime. Who could possibly believe this? [*Pause.*] No! [*He gets up.*] I won't do it. I cannot

THE REX CINEMA TRIAL 93

do this. [*To the control room, over the intercom.*] Listen, Alireza, stop everything! Don't do anything else. Pack up the equipment. We're going back. Tonight. No, tomorrow morning. Yes, we're going back. [*Begins to remove the camera from the tripod.*] This I cannot do. [*Silence.*]

HOSEYN [*turns on the tape recorder. A section of "The Little Sparrow" song, which was used at the beginning of the movie, "Gavazn-ha," is heard: "The rain will come and you'll get wet. The snow will turn you to a ball, I bet. And you'll roll into the painted pool."*[4] *The DIRECTOR looks at him.*]: It's from "Gavazn-ha." It was a good movie; I really liked it.

DIRECTOR: How far into the movie did you see before, as you say, you set the theater on fire?

HOSEYN: I had seen it before. You know, Mr. Tala'i, people count on you. [*He climbs off the stage and approaches the DIRECTOR, who is gathering up the equipment.*] These people have given so many empty answers to the families of the Rex Cinema martyrs that they don't trust them anymore. But when they heard that you were going to show the trial on television, they became hopeful. Don't disappoint them. Help the people learn the truth.

DIRECTOR: Hah! Look who's worrying about the people! Anyway, who is going to tell the truth to the people? You?

HOSEYN: I will. I'm not afraid of anybody. I'll tell all I know.

DIRECTOR: Your name isn't even on the list of defendants, poor thing. There are five primary defendants who are now in prison. If you were supposed to be put on trial, you wouldn't be walking around a free man.

HOSEYN: Well, that's why I've come to you, so you can do something for me.

DIRECTOR: Do what for you? Write you a letter of recommendation so they'll give you a job?

HOSEYN: So that they'll give me a trial. Well, I am the arsonist, not the ones that Alishahi has made a case against. None of them was in this business with me. God is my witness.

[*The DIRECTOR stares at him in silence for a while.*]

VOICE FROM THE CONTROL ROOM: Mr. Tala'i. Long distance phone call. . . .

DIRECTOR [*hurriedly*]: Is there a phone behind the stage?

VOICE OVER THE INTERCOM: Please come to the control room.

[*The DIRECTOR exits through the door in the middle of the auditorium.*]

HOSEYN: If you tell them, they'll listen to you, Mr. Tala'i. They will put me on trial. . . . [*Pause.*] He must be a good man. His movie was good. There was a scene in it that had nothing to do with the main story of the movie, but it reminded me of my brother-in-law, God rest his soul. The bridegroom faints on his wedding night. He was lying with his wedding suit on the ground in the yard. Someone was drawing a line around him and everybody else was standing by and watching. My poor sister was standing by the window and trembling like a willow. She was shaking so bad that the window was making crackling sounds. [*Pause.*] I'm not a fainter . . ., but ever since I was a kid, that is, ever since I saw my brother-in-law like that, I've always thought I would faint, too, on my wedding night and fall flat on the ground.

Act I
Scene Three

ALISHAHI comes forward from the back of the stage with files under his arm. He is dressed in unpressed trousers, an old jacket, and tennis shoes. He is bearded, and his shirt collar is open. He is no more than 35 years of age.

ALISHAHI: Mr. Tala'i?

HOSEYN: Hello, Mr. Alishahi.

ALISHAHI [*surprised to see him*]: Isn't Mr. Tala'i here?

HOSEYN: He's gone to answer the phone.

ALISHAHI [*calling out off-stage*]: Please come in here, Haj Aqa. Come in, please. [*JA'FARI hurries in. He is wearing a black turban and a black robe. He is a clergyman, under 40 years of age.*]

HOSEYN: Hello, Haj Aqa.

JA'FARI: Uh . . . what is he doing here? [*ALISHAHI shakes his head.*] What are you doing here?

HOSEYN: I came to. . . .

JA'FARI: You were supposed to go on pilgrimage. I told them to get you a ticket to Mashhad.[5] Didn't they get you one?

HOSEYN: Yes, they did, Haj Aqa. . . .

JA'FARI: Then, where is it? What did you do with the ticket?

HOSEYN: Here it is, Haj Aqa. . . . [*Puts his hand in the inside pocket of his jacket.*]

JA'FARI: Then, why didn't you go?

HOSEYN: What can I say? His Holiness didn't want me, I suppose. . . .

JA'FARI: His Holiness? What holiness?

HOSEYN: His Holiness, the Eighth Imam, the Refuge of Strangers, may my life be sacrificed for him.[6]

JA'FARI: Good God!

HOSEYN: How could I dare go, Haj Aqa? How could I touch his sacred shrine with these hands? My hands are unclean, Haj Aqa. I can't clean them off, I swear to God. . . .

JA'FARI: No. No way one can deal with this guy. [*Sits.*]

ALISHAHI: Look, my friend! What bothers you now is not guilt itself. It is feeling guilty.

[*Pause.*]

HOSEYN: What's the difference?

ALISHAHI: We all suffer from a sense of guilt, more or less. But actual guilt itself, weighing it, or even trying to decide whether or not it exists is not in our hands.

HOSEYN: You mean I haven't committed a sin? I feel like I have.

ALISHAHI: I am not talking about whether you have or have not committed a sin. Suppose you are guilty. It is not up to you to decide about it or about what punishment is due. Someone else will do that.

HOSEYN: That is exactly what I mean.

JA'FARI: Don't worry. The sin that you have committed will not go unpunished. What do you think Heaven and Hell are for? They were created so that no one will end up without reward or punishment.

HOSEYN: Then, why are you putting the others on trial? Why not let their punishment go until Judgment Day?

JA'FARI: They are considered corrupt on the basis of worldly laws. Religious and civil laws. . . .

HOSEYN: They are going to be on trial for what I have committed.

ALISHAHI: That is exactly the point, my friend. That is why I say it is not for you to decide. When your revolutionary act is put in historical perspective, it, in fact, will appear to be a proper, destiny-making, even admirable act. It was their conduct that caused this proper revolutionary act of yours to come to a tragic end, and at a specific critical point in time, for that matter. In the general process and historical continuum. . . .

HOSEYN: Mr. Alishahi, I beg you. I am not educated enough to understand what you say. When I check my own conscience. . . .

ALISHAHI: You feel sinful. I understand what you are saying. I already said that you feel guilty, didn't I?

HOSEYN: Well, that's it. That's exactly what is tormenting me.

JA'FARI: Repentance! What do you think repentance is for? Oblation, pleading, pilgrimage. These are the things that lighten your burden. Try them. If they don't work, come back to me.

HOSEYN: I will not go to Mashhad, Haj Aqa. I beg you, in the name of your ancestor, the Prophet. . . .[7] [*He returns the ticket.*]

JA'FARI [*angrily*]: Well, to hell with it. You can go to the depths of Hell. . . .

ALISHAHI: Allow me. . . .

JA'FARI: He makes my blood boil. He promised that he would not show up around here anymore. He promised he would shut his mouth.

HOSEYN: Did I. . . .

JA'FARI: If he doesn't want to go on pilgrimage, so be it. He is probably not fortunate enough and probably not worthy of it. What did he come here for?

ALISHAHI: He feels guilty.

HOSEYN: Haj Aqa. . . .

JA'FARI: I wrote a letter to that good-for-nothing Colonel. I got him out of jail. I vouched for him . . . that he was not guilty. And still he goes around saying that he is guilty!

ALISHAHI: He feels guilty.

HOSEYN: Mr. Alishahi. . . .

JA'FARI: It is my fault, Mr. Alishahi. I sent him to Esfahan with Habibollah Baziyar to see Ayatollah Khademi. I bent over backwards at the office of Ayatollah Taheri for them to do something for him, to get him busy with something there. Habibollah came back and said, "Sir, this guy can't control his tongue. . . . He makes the situation more embarrassing than it is." I sent him again to Tehran, to the office of Hashem Sabbaghian, so that maybe they would send him abroad—Dubai, Qatar, Abu Dhabi, somewhere. He made such a scene. Habibollah said that he would not go anywhere with him anymore.

ALISHAHI: Unbelievable!

HOSEYN: Habibollah himself. . . .

JA'FARI: I don't know why, instead of all this, I didn't send him to a mental asylum.

HOSEYN [*nervously*]: I am not mad. . . .

JA'FARI: You are! You are! Much worse than a madman. At least a madman wouldn't accuse himself of a crime.

ALISHAHI: Look, my friend. . . .

HOSEYN [*crying*]: But, let me say something, too, damn it.

ALISHAHI: You are really upsetting his honor.

JA'FARI: Let him talk. Let's see what he has to say. Talk!

HOSEYN: Uh. . . . [*He has forgotten.*]

JA'FARI: Then talk.

HOSEYN: I . . . you . . . what was I. . . . Aha; it was agreed that if a trial was going to take place, I, too. . . .

JA'FARI: Don't you see? This trial is your fault, too. You yourself are the main cause of this problem that has been created for us.

HOSEYN: This is what I'm saying. Why shouldn't I be in the trial?

JA'FARI: What a jackass!

ALISHAHI: Where is this Mr. Tala'i? Mr. Tala'i!

JA'FARI: All the talk about the incident had died down, Mr. Alishahi. Because of his big mouth and all the nonsense he said, the relatives of the victims started up again. They carry on sit-ins here and there. They petition to this person and that person. This is what it has come to. And now, how can we fix the mess? With all the problems in the country that have been piled on us, how can we try to quiet these people down?

HOSEYN: What I said. . . .

JA'FARI: It has nothing to do with us anyway. Something occurred during the previous tyrannical regime, and all its perpetrators have died or gone somewhere else. Do we still have to account for what they did?

HOSEYN [*helplessly and in tears*]: Your honor, I'd give my life for your ancestor. I don't feel well at all. Since the night of the Rex Cinema incident, I have lost all control of myself. I don't know night from day. I don't know when I'm asleep and when I'm awake. My sleep is just like being awake. When I'm awake, I feel like I'm being tortured. I'm not crazy; no, I'm crazy. If I were, that would be my excuse. As you said, I would put myself in a mental asylum. What makes it worse is that I have all my wits about me. I realize that I'm not well.

ALISHAHI [*in a loud voice*]: Mr. Tala'i!

HOSEYN: As God is my witness, I didn't say anything to anybody. I kept my mouth shut. When my mother saw that I was feeling so bad and couldn't sleep or eat, she went to Naneh Namaki, the women's professional mourner, and explained the situation to her, so that she could give me some sort of prayer. That's how the word got out. Now you want to make it all my fault? Okay, it's my fault. I'm not asking you for anything. I'm not asking for a position or money. All I'm asking is for you to put me with the rest and finish me off, so I'll be free.

JA'FARI: Do it yourself. Take a pill or something. Swallow a chunk of opium to finish yourself off. Why are you bothering us? Why do you want to taint the revolution, you idiot?

HOSEYN: Doesn't this revolution belong to these poor people? Well, let them know what really happened.

ALISHAHI: My friend, you don't seem to understand what's behind all this.

JA'FARI: And you don't seem to understand the main point of the matter, Mr. Alishahi. [*Pause.*] What he says is not just he himself speaking at all. They have put words in his mouth. I know this man. He can't even carry on an ordinary conversation. He can't even understand a simple idea. Don't you smell something in all he says? Don't you see the influence of associating with the minigroups?[8]

ALISHAHI: Certainly. [*Makes a note.*]

HOSEYN: You can't fool me with these things anymore. I'm going to take part in this trial that is supposed to be shown on television. I told Mr. Tala'i, too.

JA'FARI: Told whom? Ha, ha, the things one has to hear!

HOSEYN: And he promised to put me in the trial.

ALISHAHI: My simple-minded friend, the likes of Mr. Tala'i are not of the level to be able to give such promises to anyone. [*Notices the DIRECTOR enter.*] Mr. Tala'i is, of course, a distinguished artist. And his record and competence are well known. But in this trial, his responsibility is to use his creative talents to properly show this trial to the Iranian nation. As for whom is to be on trial and how he is going to be tried, that is the responsibility and within the jurisdiction of the person who has what? The handwritten instructions of the leader of the revolution? Mr. Tala'i, where have you been, my friend? A problem has come up. Hojjat al-Islam does not give his consent to hold the trial in the theater. He says it would be better to hold it in a mosque. I told him your opinion, with which I agreed, in terms of technical resources and. . . .

JA'FARI: Before bringing this matter up, allow me to ask the director a question. Mr. Tala'i, in your opinion, is this a trial or a motion picture? [*Pause.*] If you consider it a motion picture, we will leave, because I personally am by no means an actor. However, if it is not a motion picture, please do not assign roles to people. [*Pause.*]

ALISHAHI: This man claims that you have promised him a part in the trial.

HOSEYN: I said. . . .

DIRECTOR: You should first prove that you are related, as the saying goes, then you can talk about dividing the inheritance. First, see if I agree to work with you on this silly show; then you can interrogate me about what I did or did not say to this or that person.

HOSEYN [*protesting*]: Mr. Tala'i!

ALISHAHI: It is too late for this kind of talk, my friend. The program has been announced on television and in the newspapers.

JA'FARI: You promised cooperation.

DIRECTOR: And so did you. I set my conditions from the beginning, didn't I?

JA'FARI: Why are you going back on your word now?

DIRECTOR: I was just talking to Tehran. My wife has been summoned to Evin Prison again. You were supposed to talk to them.

JA'FARI: I did.

DIRECTOR: You talked to them! And it sure did a lot of good!

JA'FARI: Where did your wife spend the night last night? Did she go home or not?

DIRECTOR: Obviously.

JA'FARI: Which shows that I talked to them and it did do some good.

DIRECTOR [*pauses*]: Did you expect them not to let her go home? Has she committed a crime?

JA'FARI: Don't you understand? It is a revolution, my dear sir. There has been a revolution.

DIRECTOR: You don't need to remind me that there has been a revolution. You should be reminded of it. I am the one who created the revolution.

JA'FARI. If you created it, don't try to ruin it. Respect it. Let the offender answer for what he has done, even if it is yourself.

DIRECTOR: My wife has not committed any offense. She just sang. And she sang well, too.

JA'FARI: But she sang.

DIRECTOR: It was her job. My job was to make movies. Your job was to preach. This man's job [*referring to ALISHAHI*] was, I don't know, to shine shoes. They constantly ask her why she sang here or why she sang there, why she sang this way and didn't sing that way. When you were asked to preach, did you ask if the businessman who had invited you had made his money legitimately or not? If someone sent shoes to this man's shop to be shined, would he ask if they belonged to a smuggler or a highway robber?

JA'FARI: Are all professions the same to you? Is there no difference between an old woman who weaves carpets and a SAVAK torturer?

DIRECTOR: This kind of ridiculous classification. . . .

ALISHAHI: Excuse me. By the way, I did not shine shoes.

DIRECTOR: Then, what? What did you do?

ALISHAHI: I was a teacher.

DIRECTOR: Where did you teach, in Saint Germaine District in Paris?

ALISHAHI: No, in Naziabad.

DIRECTOR: Obviously. Which ministry paid your salary? Our own Ministry of Education? Who was the minister? This same woman who was executed some time ago by this gentleman [*referring to JA'FARI*] or the guy who was executed a few weeks before? Well, why shouldn't you be put on trial? After all, so far, two ministers from your ministry have been executed. My wife didn't even have one. In fact, she wasn't part of any ministry.

JA'FARI: A false analogy!

ALISHAHI: But I didn't go to Amjadiyyeh on every Aban 4,[9] the Shah's birthday. I didn't line up the students to take them to the airport to welcome the U.S. president. I didn't wave a flag on the street when His Majesty's motorcade went by....

DIRECTOR: You were an intellectual! You were in the opposition! You didn't kiss ass! I know what you were. You sat and listened to Shari'ati's speeches at the Hoseyniyyeh Ershad.[10] You used to cheer the poets at the Goethe Institute on poetry evenings, even if their poems were mediocre and without substance.[11] When you confuse all these things together, then the conclusion is that other teachers who were not doing the same were bad. You were good because you were as you were. Just for the sake of argument, I will agree with this conclusion. There are good teachers and bad teachers. Then, let us not differentiate between individuals on the basis of their professions. Let us agree that in the most undesirable of jobs, which today we think of as working for SAVAK, someone might be ethical and act as a human being, within his own limits, and that in the most noble of professions, such as teaching or preaching, especially in preaching, there might be individuals who would not hesitate to commit any treacherous, heinous, criminal act.

JA'FARI: Does this rule apply as well to the so-called artists, or doesn't it?

DIRECTOR: Of course it does.

JA'FARI: Is your wife an artist or not?

DIRECTOR: Why do they take her to Evin for interrogation? Interrogation for what?

JA'FARI: Are you against interrogations?

DIRECTOR: That motherfucker, your colleague, asks my wife whether she has slept with anyone other than her husband.

JA'FARI: Well, she can say no, if the answer is indeed in the negative.

DIRECTOR: Why in the world...? Why should such an obscene question be asked at all? What gives them the right?

ALISHAHI: Look, my friend!

JA'FARI: Permit me, sir. I still don't understand what this gentleman is objecting to. To the interrogation of artists or the interrogation of his wife?

DIRECTOR: Both. Both. Why should anyone be interrogated at all? Artist or no artist. The goal of the revolution is not to ask people whether or not they wash themselves after going to the bathroom! There was a revolution in order to replace a corrupt system with a better one. You establish that better system, and the social machine will automatically begin to work towards betterment.

ALISHAHI: How can a better system be established when the former corrupt elements continue their corruption?

DIRECTOR: Who decides what is corrupt and how? How do we know the judge is not more corrupt than those he judges as corrupt? If you were to interrogate people for every move they made, you would need as many judges as there are people. Where will you find all those judges? The revolution is just taking its first breath. It is still in its infancy. No new criteria for discrimination and evaluation have yet been created. When the tools for establishing justice are still so imperfect, why do you insist on using this as a pretext to harass the people, who are supposed to enjoy, God forbid, the benefits of this revolution? Well, the result is what you have: this trial that you have set up.

JA'FARI: Then you oppose any revolutionary trial.

DIRECTOR: Why say revolutionary? Say phony.

ALISHAHI: My friend, you are. . . .

DIRECTOR: Please, don't keep patronizing me with "my friend." I am by no means your friend. Who do you think you are anyway? What kind of education or qualifications do you have to be the prosecutor in this trial? All ceremonies aside. As for this gentleman himself [*referring to JA'FARI*], who, up to a few days ago, used to sing about the martyrdom of Ali Akbar, what are his qualifications to preside over this trial, for that matter, a trial that is so sensitive and, as you say, destiny-making?[12] Really, by what authority do you preside over this trial?

JA'FARI: The Imam's handwritten decree.

ALISHAHI: Bravo!

[*Pause.*]

DIRECTOR: The Imam's handwritten decree. The Imam's handwritten decree can assign you the task. That is correct. But does it also give you sufficient knowledge and expertise to face the important task that is before you? What does your conscience tell you?

JA'FARI: If His Eminence had not found me to be competent, he would not have given me the handwritten decree.

[*Pause.*]

DIRECTOR: His Eminence did not give me a handwritten decree, did he? Then, I must bid you farewell. [*Begins to gather up the equipment.*] I'll go back. If your colleague summons my wife once more, this time I will go with her and put a bullet in his head, which is full of cow dung. It is revolution, after all. Anything goes.

HOSEYN: Mr. Tala'i. Take it easy, for God's sake. Let this trial begin. God willing, your wife's problems will be resolved.

ALISHAHI: Do you really intend to leave?

[*JA'FARI smiles sarcastically.*]

DIRECTOR: Who is going to stop me?

ALISHAHI: What do you think?

DIRECTOR: I think this ridiculous show is not the kind of thing I can do.

JA'FARI: Ridiculous show?

ALISHAHI: Allow me, please. [*To the DIRECTOR*] You are wearing a gun on your belt; I am not. You are wearing boots; I am not. You claim that you started the revolution; I do not. All of these mean that you are much more of a revolutionary than I am.

DIRECTOR: Conclusion?

ALISHAHI: Then, why do you try to pretend that you don't understand the revolutionary exigency of this trial?

DIRECTOR: Revolutionary exigency! Very interesting! Revolutionary exigency means that this guy [*referring to HOSEYN*], the main culprit in the Rex Cinema crime, walks around free and clear. And even when he is accidentally caught, they take him out of jail. Then they put several other people on trial who had practically no hand in the setting of the fire! Is this revolutionary exigency?

ALISHAHI: Yes.

HOSEYN: You've got to be kidding!

DIRECTOR [*backing HOSEYN*]: Really!

ALISHAHI: This person's name is Hoseyn Takbe'alizadeh. That is, he is an individual. Here we are not dealing with an individual. Here a system must be put on trial, not individuals.

HOSEYN: What is he talking about?

DIRECTOR: Allow me. Who are these people who are supposed to be tried? Don't they have birth certificates? Does the birth certificate of each one of them represent more than one individual?

ALISHAHI: Each one of them is a unit within the framework of the previous system, against which the revolution took place. They worked for it. But all of them together represent the operation of a system that included the Rex Cinema incident as one of its results.

DIRECTOR: And this man is not involved at all? [*referring to HOSEYN*]

ALISHAHI: Within the framework that is intended, he is not involved at all.

DIRECTOR: And must not be tried?

ALISHAHI: And must not be tried!

[*Pause.*]

HOSEYN: Mr. Alishahi, pardon me, but you are a real motherfucker!

JA'FARI: Shame on you! Watch your language!

HOSEYN: I swear on your life, I know what I am saying, Haj Aqa. This guy is a motherfucker. And there's no doubt about it.

JA'FARI: He is being impudent again. How obscene. Really, biting the hand that feeds you!?

HOSEYN: You can take back the medal you gave me.

JA'FARI: Call a guard; have him taken away.

ALISHAHI: Don't upset yourself, Haj Aqa. Let him say whatever he wants. Time is really running out. If this trial is postponed for whatever reason or is not televised, it will give the counterrevolutionaries an opportunity to spread rumors. Allow the trial to take place right here in this auditorium. There is really no time to have the mosque prepared for it. And don't worry about the security. The whole place has been thoroughly inspected, and guards are in place. It is true that the theater is reserved exclusively for the families and relatives of the victims of the incident, but our own agents are also among them.

JA'FARI: But, my dear sir, I want to recite *hadiths*; I want to recite verses from the Koran. Here, for many years, unveiled women with bare heads and breasts watched uncensored movies. It is not the proper place for it.

ALISHAHI: But your statements will be televised from a place where they used to spread immorality and corrupting ideas.

JA'FARI: What if they say some nonsense they shouldn't say? Everything will be televised.

ALISHAHI: We have spoken to the people in charge of the broadcast. In places where something inappropriate occurs, they are supposed to fill in with slides, commercials, and committee communiques. Nevertheless, to be ready for anything we have also prepared several kinds of tapes to be broadcast when the trial is politically moving away from its proper course. Of course, the practical aspects should be left to the Director to decide. [*To the DIRECTOR*] Do you want to listen to them?

DIRECTOR: We all must take lessons from you in this kind of work. By the way, don't talk as if I've agreed to cooperate.

ALISHAHI: You will! You will cooperate.

HOSEYN: No, Mr. Tala'i. No going back on your word. So far, I have been with you. But from here on, I'm not.

DIRECTOR: You keep quiet.

HOSEYN: You promised you wouldn't back out.

DIRECTOR: I didn't give any promises to anyone.

JA'FARI: You gave us your word. You promised to cooperate.

DIRECTOR: Especially to you, I did not give any promise. Qotbzadeh saddled me with this business.[13]

JA'FARI: What difference does it make? He works for us. We all work for the revolution.

ALISHAHI: Does this mean that you are willing to sacrifice the directorship of Network Two and being deputy to Mr. Qotbzadeh, which you were promised for this business?[14]

DIRECTOR: Is that what you think? If I had been interested in status and position; my dear sir, not only did I have much better opportunities during the previous regime, but I deserved them too.

JA'FARI: He won't leave, sir. He won't. He is putting a high price on himself.

HOSEYN: Yes, he is bluffing.

JA'FARI: He knows that if he leaves, he is no longer one of us.

DIRECTOR: I never was.

JA'FARI: He knows that if he leaves, I won't call Tehrani in Evin Prison, who won't have his wife sent home before he gets there and before a bullet has been fired into her.

DIRECTOR: Is this a threat?

JA'FARI: It is a fact. If you and I are not servants of the revolution, there is no reason for them to treat us differently.

THE REX CINEMA TRIAL 109

[*Silence. All three stare at him.*]

DIRECTOR: All three of you guessed right. I will cooperate.

[*ALISHAHI and JA'FARI smile and nod, and HOSEYN shows his excitement.*]

HOSEYN: Way to go, Mr. Tala'i; way to go!

DIRECTOR: But I am against you.

HOSEYN: Come on, now!

DIRECTOR: And, after all this is over, I will settle my account with you.

JA'FARI: We will all settle our accounts. Of course.

ALISHAHI: That's life.

DIRECTOR [*referring to HOSEYN*]: And this person will also be put on trial.

HOSEYN: Bless your heart.

ALISHAHI: No!

DIRECTOR: With the primary defendants.

ALISHAHI: No!

HOSEYN: What do you mean no? Who is this guy anyway?

JA'FARI: Quiet!

ALISHAHI: The general policy of this trial, as I said, is to try to condemn the previous system. [*To the DIRECTOR*] You might not like what I say. According to this policy, you, personally, deserve more to sit in with the primary defendants.

[*Silence.*]

DIRECTOR: No. Wait a minute. I seem to have missed something. What were you saying?

ALISHAHI: Is it really necessary for me to explain?

DIRECTOR: Please do! Do me a favor and do so!

ALISHAHI: If I am not mistaken, a few minutes ago, you claimed that you personally started the revolution.

DIRECTOR: It is not a claim.

ALISHAHI: It is an absolute fact! But how? How did you start the revolution? In what way?

DIRECTOR: With my work. With my films.

ALISHAHI: Which one? Can you name a specific film?

DIRECTOR: Well, all of them. Despite the lack of resources and their weaknesses, any one of them you might choose was an engine, a driving force, in the course of the revolution. This is not just a claim. They are there. You can watch them on the screen.

HOSEYN: Mr. Tala'i, take it easy, brother. I've seen all of your movies, except for the first one, what was it called. . . ?

DIRECTOR: "Come Stranger."

HOSEYN: Yes, except for that one, and the other one that you made with Fardin.[15] Some of them, between us—I don't know about engines—they were more like brakes.

DIRECTOR: For instance, Mr. Film Critic?

HOSEYN: Don't be offended. I am on your side. For example, what was that one—"Tatam Ratam Datam Look at That Drummer!" Was that an engine?

JA'FARI [*laughing*]: What? What did you say it was called?

HOSEYN [*encouraged*]: "Tatam Ratam Datam Look at That Drummer," "The Fiddler with Glasses Marching with That Drummer!"[16]

JA'FARI [*bursting out laughing*]: As far as being a drummer is concerned, Mr. Director, your own friend told us what kind of drummer you are.

THE REX CINEMA TRIAL   111

[*Silence.*]

DIRECTOR [*after looking at HOSEYN for a moment*]: You enjoyed it, didn't you?

HOSEYN: Who? Me?

DIRECTOR: Yes. Didn't you enjoy the piece that you were imitating just now?

HOSEYN: Yes. I did, very much. I saw it twice. Wasn't it called "Qeysar?" I saw it twice. [*To JA'FARI*] That was, when I wasn't coming to the religious meetings to see you.

DIRECTOR: The purpose of that particular piece was to entertain people like you, and for people unlike you to see how people like you entertain themselves. Every good film is like a crystal ball. You can see everything in it. It depends on the angle from which you are looking at it.

ALISHAHI: Let's not get into a discussion about art. And nobody here doubts your talents as an artist. The question is: If you, as an engine of the revolution, were going to choose one of your movies, which one would it be?

[*Pause.*]

DIRECTOR: "The Journey of Stone."

HOSEYN: That's the one.

DIRECTOR: Before the film was released, I showed it to several people in the theological center, [*to JA'FARI*] to your own colleagues. I arranged a private showing for them. The people from Hoseyniyyeh Ershad came, too. When the film was over, they all said: "That is it. After this movie, the whole thing will be over. With this, the people will pour into the streets." And they did.

ALISHAHI: You are right. That film was effective in exciting people's religious and ideological sentiments, especially with the scenes about religious mourning ceremonies and chest-beating. But if I were you, I would have chosen "Gavazn-ha."

DIRECTOR: "Gavazn-ha." Yes, I told you, you can choose any one of them. What cat-and-mouse games I had to play with the censors about that film! Several times they forced us to change the ending, and what finally went on the screen was not at all what I had originally made.

HOSEYN: I love the scene where the bridegroom faints on his wedding night.

DIRECTOR: If you take a poll, you will see that more people saw this movie than "The Journey of Stone"; it was around longer. Right here in Abadan, it was shown fives times in three years, and each time for several weeks. Still, the night of the Rex Cinema fire, the theater was full.

HOSEYN [*uneasy*]: Yes. Even though it was the last show.

DIRECTOR: Even though it was the last show. When the Rex Cinema showed a rerun, especially at the last show, it hardly had two or three rows of spectators. But, for "Gavazn-ha," . . . and it was its fifth showing . . . the last show, the theater, which was never full, was filled with spectators. [*Pause.*] The people were ripe for it. [*Pause.*] They had caught on to the ideas. Those ideas were theirs. It was what was in their hearts. [*Silence.*] Why are you looking at me like that? I didn't make the movie for the people to be burned alive when they were watching it. I made movies to commiserate with them. I made movies for their freedom.

JA'FARI: Did you want to kill the people, Hoseyn? Out with it; talk. Did you set the theater on fire to burn the people?

HOSEYN: No, sir, I swear on your holy ancestor. I'm human, too, sir. [*Weeps.*] I have a heart, too, sir. I'm not Shemr ebn-e zel-Jowshan, you know.[17] I started to shout "fire" before anyone else, so that they would let them out the exit door. We didn't know the doors would lock by themselves and the electricity would cut off. We shouldn't have gone there, anyway, because the theater was full. When all those people rushed to the door, they were trampled underfoot. Oh, I wish it would have been on some other night, in some other theater, some other movie, where there were no more than two or three rows of people who could have gotten out in time.

[*Silence.*]

ALISHAHI [*calmly and deliberately*]: If it had been another night or another movie and there had been seventy people instead of three hundred

THE REX CINEMA TRIAL

seventy, supposing that all of them had burned, only seventy would have burned. Now, your share in your revolution's engine is three hundred burned corpses more! Are you prepared to talk about it on the stand with the primary defendants?

DIRECTOR [*after a long pause*]: Why not? It is only in your revolution that one has to suffer punishment for his good deeds, too.

ALISHAHI: Up to a few minutes ago, it was your revolution. You had started it. But now, it is our revolution!

VOICE OVER THE INTERCOM: Hojjat al-Islam Ja'fari-Tabrizi, telephone!

JA'FARI: Where?

VOICE: Internal line. You can talk backstage. [*JA'FARI exits.*]

[*Silence.*]

DIRECTOR: I understand him [*referring to JA'FARI*], and I understand this one, too [*referring to HOSEYN*], but I don't understand you.

ALISHAHI: They are not complicated people. They are one-dimensional, like the workers in your movies. They are easy to understand. But, if you understand me, someday you'll make better movies, with multi-dimensional characters, like real people.

JA'FARI'S VOICE [*from outside*]: Where is this telephone?

[*ALISHAHI goes to help.*]

DIRECTOR [*to HOSEYN*]: You said the right thing to this guy.

HOSEYN: He is a motherfucker. And he won't put me in the trial. [*Looks around.*] But I won't give up. I'll mess up all their plans.

DIRECTOR: They will have guards everywhere. Didn't you hear what he said?

HOSEYN: They're no match for me in this business. I've had a lot of experience. Are you serious or not? Should we do it?

DIRECTOR: Do what?

HOSEYN: Blow it up, right during the trial, so that they go up in smoke, all of them!

[*Pause.*]

DIRECTOR: What about the people? You are still suffering from a guilty conscience for what you did. Is your guilty conscience fake too? Who do you think the people are who will gather here? Relatives of the Rex Cinema victims. Have you no shame? They haven't gotten over the other tragedy yet.

HOSEYN: I'm sorry. I said something stupid again.

DIRECTOR: Listen! I can't persist on your behalf more than I have. But wait here, let's see what happens. It is a revolution after all. Anything can happen at any moment. Something might work out.

HOSEYN: If I know these people, they won't even let me sit in the audience.

DIRECTOR: I'll tell them I need you to help me. Just stand by my side.

HOSEYN: Much obliged to you, Mr. Tala'i. Let me kiss your hand.

DIRECTOR: Let go of my hand. Just don't pester me; keep your mouth shut; and stay close to me. If you leave my sight, they might do you in.

HOSEYN: Don't even think about it. From now on, I'll follow you like a shadow.

DIRECTOR: Close the curtain.

[*As the curtain is being closed, the DIRECTOR exits, followed by HOSEYN.*]

Act II
Scene One

The defendants are now sitting among the audience. The DIRECTOR, with a TV camera on his shoulder, makes his way around the theater auditorium, towards the stage. While taking care to avoid the cords wrapping around people's legs, HOSEYN follows the DIRECTOR with a flashlight. He apologizes to people and greets a couple of people, including the MANAGER OF THE THEATER. LIEUTENANT BAHMANI recognizes him.

LIEUTENANT: Hoseyn, you've come up in the world. You are installing cables.

HOSEYN [*shyly*]: One's got to do something, Captain. Mr. Tala'i was kind enough to arrange this for me. [*Places his hand at the side of his mouth, trying to explain to whom he is referring and whispers*] "Gavazn-ha."

LIEUTENANT: I know him; I know him. I've seen his movies. And I've gotten to know him better personally, recently. We've gotten to know a lot of people we didn't know that well in the past, and will get to know them even better.

HOSEYN: How is it going?

LIEUTENANT: Fine, of course. Let the enemies of this country eat their hearts out. I couldn't be better. Mr. Director, are you also one of those who will be conducting the trial?

DIRECTOR: No, sir. I have no official part in the trial. I am just taping the trial for broadcast on TV.

LIEUTENANT: Is that right? You are now sweeping up the road that you paved for these people to take over the government.

[*A GUARD in civilian clothes and military helmet approaches him and whispers something to him.*]

OWNER OF THE THEATER: Sir, are you now going to televise whatever is said in this trial? You mean, it won't be censored?

DIRECTOR: I have no idea. I am just taping the trial. Whether it is going to be shown, or how much of it will be shown, to tell you the truth, I don't know.

HOSEYN: Let me tell you. Not all of it will be shown. But whatever is shown is better than nothing being shown at all.

[*The DIRECTOR pulls him aside and signals for him not to talk to the audience. The curtain opens with the anthem of the Islamic Republic. The stage has been set for the trial. The JUDGE's desk and chair are placed at an angle to the left and the PROSECUTOR's desk and chair are on the right. In the middle stands a podium on a platform, to elevate the defendants even more than the JUDGE and the PROSECUTOR. A floor plan of the Rex Cinema building is hung behind the podium on a white board. There is a book with a green cover on the JUDGE's desk and a tape recorder and several files on the PROSECUTOR's desk. The PROSECUTOR, with a piece of paper in his hand, is standing prepared from the beginning, on center front stage. After the curtain has opened and the anthem is finished, he reads off the piece of paper. He is seen on the monitors, which have been installed earlier, through the DIRECTOR's camera.*]

ALISHAHI: Moslem brothers and sisters. This is your trial.

LIEUTENANT: Meaning, you will all be tried. Today, it is our turn, and tomorrow, the rest.

[*Some laugh and several people whisper "sh."*]

ALISHAHI: It was your willpower, through your sit-ins in the Department of Finance, followed by seeking justice in all governmental and military units, which finally instigated this historical trial to investigate the great, inhuman tragedy of the Rex Cinema. We do not need to be reminded that the tyrannical and cruel regime of the Shah, which was the perpetrator of this fire, during the few months that it had the opportunity before it was overthrown, not only took no steps to show how this horrible human incineration occurred, but did its best to destroy the evidence and documents pertaining to this tragedy. However, because the truth will not remain hidden behind the clouds forever and divine justice will finally catch up with tyrants and oppressors, despite the thousands of calamities and tragedies that were left as a legacy of the corrupt regime of the past, in accordance with the decree of the Leader of the Revolution, the investigation of this tragedy and justice for the suffering nation have been

THE REX CINEMA TRIAL

given priority over all other affairs, and the perpetrators of this crime have been arrested and are being brought to trial. These perpetrators are now sitting among you, so that in a people's revolutionary and Islamic trial they will receive punishment for the acts that they have or have not committed. Before presenting the judge of this revolutionary court, I must warn you to refrain from clapping and expressing your emotions in the manner of the past tyrannical trials, and maintain your patience and dignity, which are among the praiseworthy characteristics of the Islamic nation, throughout the trial. As the Koran says: "God is with those who are patient." And now, Hojjat al-Islam val-Moslemin al-Ja'fari al-Tabrizi, the fully authorized representative of the Leader of the Revolution, will begin the trial.

[*ALISHAHI starts his tape recorder. As the "Khomeini, Oh Imam" song comes on, JA'FARI enters. He waves his hand to calm down the imaginary singers of the song and takes his seat. Silence.*]

JA'FARI: In the tenth verse of the blessed Sura "al-Baqarah," God states: "When it is said to them, 'Make not mischief on the earth,' they say, 'Why, we only want to make peace.'" Which means, when they are told not to corrupt the earth, they say: "But we are the reformists." [*Pause. Fingering his prayer beads.*] Before turning to the case before the court, allow me to briefly inform the honorable people present that at the time of the fire—what am I saying, the human incineration at the Rex Cinema—I was preaching on the pulpit right here in this city of Abadan. I have been familiar from a distance with that sinister tragedy, and closely with the pains of you, the Moslem victims of this tragedy. For this reason, the Representative of the Truth, the Leader of the Revolution, the Imam of the People, summoned my humble self and said emphatically: "Ja'fari, you go and take over. This is a job that you can handle; go and resolve it." And so I did.

LIEUTENANT: If you sing "One Night I Was in the Desert," this regime will not need Farrokhzad as a singer at all![18]

[*Several people, including HOSEYN, laugh involuntarily, and one or two people try to hush them.*]

JA'FARI: In the name of the Almighty. In accordance with the mandatory decree of the Imam of the People and in retribution for the blood of the innocent victims, the trial will begin.

ALISHAHI: The revolutionary spirit of this court requires us to avoid long, detailed, bureaucratic red tape, paperwork, and ceremonies. I have before me the records and the minutes of the initial interrogations of the five primary defendants, but I prefer that they introduce themselves personally. They can volunteer to come here, one by one, say what they want, and defend themselves. [*Pause.*] Of course, if there are no volunteers, I will call them by name. Are there any volunteers? [*The EMPLOYEE raises his hand.*] Come up here on the stage. [*The DIRECTOR focuses the camera on the EMPLOYEE. At his signal, HOSEYN follows the EMPLOYEE with the spotlight toward the stage. He is seen on the television monitors. He is about 40 years of age and appears to be in ill health. As he is passing by the JUDGE on the stage, ALISHAHI points at the book on the desk.*] Take the oath! [*The JUDGE motions that it is not necessary. The EMPLOYEE, guided by ALISHAHI, goes to the defendants' podium.*] Take off your glasses!

EMPLOYEE: The lights bother my eyes. If it is no trouble, allow me to keep them on.

ALISHAHI: We thought SAVAK agents wore glasses only in Iranian movies [*winks at the DIRECTOR*].

JA'FARI: State your name.

EMPLOYEE: Suppose it is Hasan, son of Taqi.

JA'FARI: How about your profession. Should we suppose that too?

EMPLOYEE: Employee of the National Intelligence and Security Agency.[19]

JA'FARI: That means SAVAK?

EMPLOYEE: Yes.

JA'FARI: What is your offense?

EMPLOYEE: I haven't committed any offense.

JA'FARI: Is that so? [*To ALISHAHI*] What is the nature of this gentleman's offense?

ALISHAHI: He was transferred by SAVAK to Abadan a few days before the Rex Cinema fire. Since he has no convincing reason for this transfer and, on the other hand, everyone knows that this incident was planned and carried out by SAVAK, this defendant is accused of carrying out this filthy plot, that is, setting the Rex Cinema on fire and burning innocent people.

JA'FARI: Well, what do you have to say now?

EMPLOYEE: I have not committed any crime.

JA'FARI: You mean this gentleman is talking nonsense?

EMPLOYEE: It is not a crime for an employee to be transferred to a provincial city. In order to say that I have had a hand in the fire, you at least should have some sort of evidence, something that proves, for instance, that I procured the equipment to set the fire from somewhere, or have someone testify that I was seen at that location on the day of the incident. Neither on the day of the incident nor before or after that day have I ever been to the Rex Cinema. In fact, I don't even know where the Rex Cinema is located in this city. I still don't even know the main streets of Abadan. How could I set fire to a place without ever having seen it?

ALISHAHI: No one is claiming that you personally took explosives inside the cinema and struck the match. This could have been done by your agents.

EMPLOYEE: I was very ill on the day of the incident. A doctor came to visit me in my hotel room. I was tossing and turning in pain. One of the hotel employees got my prescription from the pharmacy. The evidence is in the file.

ALISHAHI: There was no need for you to have left the hotel room for this action to have taken place on your initiation and under your supervision. Calling a doctor and sending a hotel employee to the pharmacy could have been a diversionary tactic, could it not?

EMPLOYEE: But the doctor's diagnosis proves that I was not pretending to be sick. I have been ill for years. Look at my service record. I was even ill when I was transferred. If a doctor who is trusted by you were to examine me, it would be proven to you.

ALISHAHI: There is no need. We fully accept that you are ill. Just tell us, why would they send a sick man on a mission?

JA'FARI: And why to Abadan, and in the middle of summer, for that matter? During that month, this city is hotter than Hell. Had they sent you off to a good climate?

EMPLOYEE: They used to transfer lots of people in those days. Maybe I was less of a go-getter than others. Or maybe I had no connections. In any case, it would not have changed the main thing. Had they sent another employee to Abadan instead of me, he would be sitting here in my place today.

ALISHAHI: You said that in those days they transferred a lot of people. Why?

EMPLOYEE: With the anti-government, and especially anti-SAVAK, propaganda which had spread everywhere, employees who had been in one place for a long time and were known were not safe. So they transferred them.

ALISHAHI: There is a more important reason that you don't mention. Every agent has some friends and relatives in his own town. In those critical days, when everyone was active against the regime in some way or another, they used to send the agents to unfamiliar regions so that friendship and kinship would not prevent them from carrying out their inhumane missions.

JA'FARI: That is correct. No matter how merciless one might be, he could not set fire to a cinema or a place where his own townspeople gather because his own relatives might be among the people there.

ALISHAHI: Most of the soldiers who fired at the demonstrators on the streets of Tehran had provincial accents.

JA'FARI: Israelis, sir, Israelis. Israeli soldiers fired at the martyrs of the revolution in blood-stained shrouds. Only an illegitimate bastard could take up arms against his fellow believers and compatriots.

ALISHAHI: Were other agents who were sent to other cities also instructed, as you were, to set fire to or set explosives in places where people assembled?

EMPLOYEE: As far as I know, no one had such a mission. Our duty was to identify the perpetrators of unrest and terrorism anywhere we were and to report it. Our duty was to keep peace and order, not to disrupt it.

THE REX CINEMA TRIAL 121

JA'FARI: It was under this pretext of "keeping the peace" that you tortured and killed the faithful and the most patriotic young people of this country!

EMPLOYEE: The people you call patriotic today were, up until some time ago, recognized as opponents of public security, according to the laws of this country. Besides, compared to the way you treat us, they were treated quite well. And, no offense intended, we, too, loved, and still love, our country.

JA'FARI: Oh, oh, oh. Do you expect a bonus and an increase in salary too? How about a medal?

EMPLOYEE: I expect nothing but death from you. I don't know why you are wasting your time talking to me. You don't need a reason to kill me. It is enough to say that I was a SAVAK agent. People despise this term so much nowadays that they don't need to know anything else. And it doesn't make any difference to them whether the man was a torturer or in charge of the pantry. As soon as you say SAVAK agent, you are allowed to take his life.

JA'FARI: There is absolutely no doubt about your guilt. The only difference between us is that you killed defenseless people without a trial, and we are giving you a chance to defend yourself. Moreover, we thought that perhaps seeing the survivors of the Rex Cinema victims would awaken your sleeping conscience, and you would identify those who cooperated with you in committing this crime.

ALISHAHI: Or at least admit what everyone agrees on, and confess that SAVAK was involved in this affair.

EMPLOYEE: It was not. It makes no sense for SAVAK to have been involved in setting the fire. The government was trying to establish calm at any price. Don't you remember? Every group that went on strike was granted anything it asked for. Anyone who made a protest was listened to, and an effort was made to appease him, not through violence, but gently and with flexibility. All this was just to keep the peace and for the people to quietly return to their work. Would they then set fire to a cinema, and one with so many people in it? That would be suicide.

ALISHAHI: That's right. That would be suicide. The previous regime was so desperate that it tried to commit suicide.

JA'FARI: And died as a result.

ALISHAHI: An attempt to commit suicide is not always actually made with the intention of suicide. Sometimes it is a pretense, or it is done to make those around the person who has tried to commit suicide give in to his demands.

JA'FARI: A person in love might try to commit suicide in order to appeal to the heart of the cruel beloved. But sometimes the beloved doesn't return, or the taxi which is taking the lover to the hospital gets stuck in traffic and the lover arrives in Hell instead of at the hospital.

EMPLOYEE: What does all this have to do with the issue at hand? What is all this talk about the lover and the beloved?

JA'FARI: The lover is the government and the beloved is the nation, the country, power.

EMPLOYEE: Those others wanted to gain power and take over the government. The government that was in power at that time had control over the country.

JA'FARI: Well, the beloved was being disloyal. The nation had begun to be difficult. And as you say, no matter how the government tried to appease her, it would not work.

ALISHAHI: The fascist government of Hitler had its agents set the Reichstag on fire in order to drive its opponents off the scene; and by making a case against others, it blamed the crime on the leftist faction. Through this device, it sent three thousand members of the German Communist Party to the firing squad. The motive of the former government in setting the Rex Cinema on fire is also quite clear. When it saw that it was losing control and was not able to control the situation, it committed this crime in order to make the people skeptical about the opposition that it called "terrorists." And its calculations were correct, to some extent, because the people saw, to a degree, that the opposition occasionally engaged in terrorist acts and setting fire to banks, government establishments, and, in some cases, cinemas—of course, without the audience. Yes, by setting the Rex Cinema on fire, the regime, in fact, fired the last fatal shot. But since luck was with the suffering Iranian nation. . . .

JA'FARI: And the Moslem nation.

ALISHAHI: And the Moslem nation, the bullet ricocheted and hit the government in the temple. I have nothing else to add.

JA'FARI: How about you? Have you anything else to add?

[*Silence.*]

EMPLOYEE: What you said may convince the people who hate the former government today, but they don't convince me, and they are not true. In any case, as I said, you don't need to provide any evidence in order to kill me. In your opinion today, we are bad; we are guilty; we are the enemy of the people; and we are whatever you say we are. Therefore, do your duty . . . and the sooner, the better. [*Pause.*] Just know this: Your turn will also come.

JA'FARI [*addressing the audience*]: How about you? Does anyone have anything to say for or against this person? [*Silence.*] I am not the only judge here, you know. Every one of you is a judge, and here you have the right to say whatever you want for or against the offenders for the retribution of the blood of your loved ones!

LIEUTENANT: If there were any justice and truth in these claims that you make, before everyone else, you should have sat where the accused is sitting and been interrogated.

JA'FARI: I thank you very much for your kindness.

OWNER OF THE THEATER: My dear sir, this kind of talk will lead to nothing but making everything worse. . . .

LIEUTENANT: What is it to you? Didn't he say himself to everyone that they should say what they have to say?

JA'FARI: I was talking about the people, who have for years made these poor people suffer.

LIEUTENANT: Now we see what you are doing to the same people! We won't be alive to see, but those who are will.

OWNER OF THE THEATER: Please, allow me. . . .

LIEUTENANT: What is it to you, anyway? Isn't that something? [*To a GUARD who has approached him*] Stand back! Don't touch me!

THEATER OF DIASPORA

[*ALISHAHI starts the tape player. Voices of a group of people. "He must be executed. This agent of corruption must be executed. This SAVAK agent must be executed." In order to neutralize the sound of ALISHAHI's tape player, HOSEYN starts his own. The "Little Sparrow" song is heard. And he sings along, encouraging others to sing. On stage, a GUARD leads the EMPLOYEE out. Because of the sound of the tape recorders, the argument between the LIEUTENANT and the OWNER OF THE THEATER cannot be heard. ALISHAHI turns off the tape player. Upon a signal from the DIRECTOR, HOSEYN also stops singing and turns off his tape player.*]

OWNER OF THE THEATER: This will finally force them to make it a secret trial. That is what I am afraid of.

ALISHAHI: Will the primary defendant, Lieutenant Bahmani, come on the stage, please.

LIEUTENANT: You asked for volunteers to come. At the present, I do not volunteer. Have you given up showing off so soon? Is this how you want to pretend to be democratic?

OWNER OF THE THEATER: What difference does it make who goes first, who second?

LIEUTENANT: If it doesn't, you go first. You are also a primary defendant, aren't you?

OWNER OF THE THEATER: All right, okay, I'll go. I volunteer. Are you satisfied? [*He goes toward the stage. The DIRECTOR follows him with the camera.*] What's happened to us? After all, we are supposed to be compatriots. We are part of the same homeland!

LIEUTENANT: Kiss ass! Go on, kiss! Let's see where it gets you. [*Sits.*]

Act II
Scene Two

OWNER OF THE THEATER [*goes on stage*]: Here you are, sir. Put me on trial. If you are going to do something to us, do it to me first. Let that gentleman breathe for half an hour longer.

ALISHAHI: Over there, please. . . .

OWNER OF THE THEATER: What is my offense? Just say it as it is; we don't have to stand on ceremony.

ALISHAHI: You are accused of. . . .

OWNER OF THE THEATER: Let me say it myself. We don't have to stand on ceremony. I am accused of being the owner of the theater. The building and the land of the theater that these ungodly ones set on fire belonged to me. Now, do I have to sit with the primary defendants just because the property belonged me? Is this fair?

ALISHAHI: Would you please go to the defendant's seat. . . .

OWNER OF THE THEATER [*without paying attention to this signal, turns to JA'FARI*]: You proved it here yourself. This was an act committed by SAVAK. Well, God bless you. What have I done wrong in the middle of all this? What do I have to do with SAVAK? What does SAVAK have to do with me?

JA'FARI: Calm down. . . . Please go to the defendant's seat.

OWNER OF THE THEATER [*heated and with fervor*]: I won't sit there, sir. Even if you draw and quarter me, I won't sit where that SAVAK agent was sitting. For God's sake, differentiate between people. Am I on the same level as that guy?

ALISHAHI: You don't even allow. . . .

OWNER OF THE THEATER: No. Is this an improper request? Am I, whose property was set on fire, and he, who set it on fire, both guilty? Are we both accused of the same thing? Is this law? Where is the law? Is it written in the Koran? Where in the Koran is it written?

JA'FARI: Don't mention the Koran by name, sir. . . .

OWNER OF THE THEATER: Why shouldn't I? I am a Moslem. All my ancestors were Moslems.

JA'FARI: You haven't taken an oath yet.

OWNER OF THE THEATER: I will, I will. [*Hurriedly picks up the book off the desk and kisses it.*]

JA'FARI [*grabs the book away from him*]: Don't touch the book, sir.

OWNER OF THE THEATER: Well, I'm taking an oath. I'll take an oath on the word of God that I am innocent. I swear by all the thirty sections of it that I didn't have anything to do with the operation of the theater at all. The property belongs to me. That is right. The whole shopping center belongs to me. But I don't know who the store keepers are. I couldn't even tend to its financial affairs and accounting. I didn't have the time. I haven't been to Abadan for three years. You have questioned the workers in the theater, haven't you?

ALISHAHI: You are not a resident of Abadan at all.

OWNER OF THE THEATER: That is right. I am not. I am from Tehran. My home, my family, everything is in Tehran.

ALISHAHI: But your cinema is in Abadan!

OWNER OF THE THEATER: Is this a crime too? Why am I being tried here? Because I have property in Abadan, or for having had a hand in the fire at the cinema? The Eighth Imam, God bless his soul, has property and endowments in the four corners of the world and throughout this country. Is there anything wrong with that?

JA'FARI: Why do you bring in the names of those we hold sacred?

OWNER OF THE THEATER: May I be struck mute! I was just giving an analogy. I want to say that a landlord does not necessarily live where he has property. No matter which city you go to, its major landfills are either in Tehran, Europe, or the United States. At least I make a living here and spend it right here. How many prayer leaders do you want me to name who have real estate in holy Najaf, which is in another country?

JA'FARI [*angrily*]: You don't need to name anyone.

OWNER OF THE THEATER: Okay, I won't. I won't name them. But is it true or not? After all, I am a bazaar merchant in some respects. I have paid my dues, *khoms* and *zakat* religious taxes.[20] I know about the ins and outs of lots of things. If it is a crime to be a landlord, then most people in this country are guilty. You might even be....

JA'FARI [*shouts*]: You are not guilty of being a landlord at all, sir.

OWNER OF THE THEATER: Then, what am I being accused of?

JA'FARI: The evidence is there. [*Points to ALISHAHI's desk.*]

OWNER OF THE THEATER: What evidence? [*Goes toward ALISHAHI.*] Show the evidence against me. Tell me why I am being tried here.

[*Pause.*]

ALISHAHI: Pardon me! You are not being tried here; we are.

OWNER OF THE THEATER: Not really. Show it to me. What am I guilty of, except being a landlord?

ALISHAHI: Greed.

OWNER OF THE THEATER: Greed? [*Pause.*] Suppose I am greedy. And very greedy. And I agree that it is a very bad thing. But, since when is being greedy a crime?

JA'FARI: Greed is one of the most heinous of actions, but when it leads to the destruction and burning of a bunch of innocent people, then it is considered a cardinal sin and a first-degree crime.

OWNER OF THE THEATER: It is still not clear to me whether SAVAK or I is supposed to have set the theater on fire.

ALISHAHI: SAVAK did it. But if you had built a better building, that is, if you had done it properly, there would not have been so many casualties, if any.

OWNER OF THE THEATER: I am not a builder, sir! Supposing that there was something wrong with the building—and, according to the City Hall permit, there was nothing wrong—the architect and the construction engineer would be guilty, not the landlord of the building.

ALISHAHI: We are not arguing about terms with you here. No architect or planner works without the approval of the landlord. Did you not know that insulation material was used in the walls of the auditorium?

OWNER OF THE THEATER: Suppose that I did not. This is a common practice, especially in Abadan. They use insulation in the walls to protect against heat and in order to keep the cool air in the building longer. This is done for conservation of energy.

ALISHAHI: To save, yes. According to the report of Colonel Amini, who is also among the primary defendants present here, the insulation in the walls accelerated the fire, making it difficult to contain in the early stages, and also, because it emitted toxic gas and smoke in the first minutes, it resulted in the suffocation of the audience, making it impossible for most of them to make an effort to reach the exit door. Why did all this happen? For what you call conservation, I call greed!

OWNER OF THE THEATER: I am telling you, this is a common practice here, everywhere. How many buildings do you want me to show you, right here in Abadan, in which insulation is used? If my property had not been set on fire, nobody would even have gotten a scratch. What fault is it of mine for having had the bad luck to have these bastards single out my theater for their plan?

ALISHAHI: Your great bad luck, in fact, is that the revolution happened. Before the revolution, nobody would come to bother you; and if they did, you would use every trick or bribe to whitewash the whole matter and leave.

OWNER OF THE THEATER: All right, there has been a revolution, as you say. A revolution is like an earthquake. If an earthquake happens and destroys houses, should the landlords of the buildings that are destroyed be arrested and executed?

ALISHAHI: In an earthquake, not all the houses are damaged the same way. There are more casualties in some and fewer in others. And the ones that have more casualties are those that have been built by building contractors like you, who don't build them properly. If there are real laws in an earthquake-stricken city, or if there is a revolution in that city, such as we

THE REX CINEMA TRIAL 129

have now, the blood of the people who have been the victims of the negligence of a bunch of greedy landlords must be avenged.

OWNER OF THE THEATER: I am no match for you in arguing. At least let me get an attorney.

JA'FARI: He even claims not to be able to argue, poor thing!

ALISHAHI: Unfortunately, you are being tried in a revolutionary court, my dear sir. Here there are no books and files, or attorneys and clerks that you might want to bribe under the table. Let me remind you again, there has been a revolution!

OWNER OF THE THEATER: What kind of thing is this to say, sir? There has been a revolution so that individuals such as myself get our rights, not to have our rights violated. There has been a revolution so that a few favorite big-shot contractors cannot control all the profitable construction projects in the country. There has been a revolution so that there will be no discrimination in the allocation and distribution of construction materials, so that the favorite ones no longer get cement below the government price while I have to buy it on the open market at three times the government rate. There has been a revolution so that in a production factory or for imported merchandise, I will not have to give shares to the Thousand Families and never know who my partners are and why.[21] There has been a revolution so that they will not be able to sell the uncultivated land they have taken possession of to the people, take the money for it in cash from their private bank, and send it abroad. I know myself that there has been a revolution. I participated in the marches from beginning to end. I myself am a devotee of the revolution, a servant of the revolution. I am prepared to give everything I have for the revolution. I am prepared to accept anything it dictates. But not like this. This is unjust. This is contrary to its purpose. If this is the way things are going to go, I must say, the Tyrant was a hundred times better.[22]

ALISHAHI: I am sorry that it does not suit your tastes. The revolution is good when it does not meddle with you. As the saying goes: "Death is good, but only for the neighbor."

JA'FARI: "You steal from the Moslem, and when you yourself are robbed, / You cry out that Moslem ways have disappeared."[23]

OWNER OF THE THEATER: Being a Moslem, the way you are talking about it, my dear sir, forgive me, is not really being a Moslem.

JA'FARI: Oh, really! What religious seminary did *you* go to to learn the Moslem ways, that you don't consider us Moslems?

ALISHAHI: This gentleman's interpretation of being a Moslem is like his interpretation of the revolution: There has been a revolution so that he can get cement! Cement!

OWNER OF THE THEATER: Why are you pretending to be stupid?

ALISHAHI: To save his skin, he even claims to be a servant of the revolution.

OWNER OF THE THEATER: I have no fear for my life, my dear sir. My fear is for my reputation and dignity, about which people like you have no inkling.

JA'FARI: As far as I am concerned, this gentleman's case is closed.

OWNER OF THE THEATER: Your case is closed, too. If you touch one hair on my head, you will pay for it. Every one of you will.

ALISHAHI [*pointing to offstage*]: This gentleman's case is closed.

OWNER OF THE THEATER [*addressing the auditorium*]: People! If this is the revolution you have made, woe be to you! [*To the DIRECTOR*] Don't take my picture, sir; take theirs. By now, I am known to those who should know me. Take their pictures so that people will see what rare fruits their revolution has produced.

> [*ALISHAHI turns on the tape player. The voice of a group is heard from the tape:* "This cruel person must be executed; this greedy landlord must be executed." *The OWNER OF THE THEATER walks to the tape player, turns it off, and attacks ALISHAHI. An armed GUARD enters and drags him away as he tries to beat up ALISHAHI and continues shouting slogans.*]

HOSEYN: Well, well! What a court of justice! [*Turns on his tape player and sings along.*] "Who'll catch it? His honor, the sweeper man. Who'll kill it? His honor, the butcher man. Who'll cook it? His honor, the cooker man."

JA'FARI [*hurriedly returns to the stage. He signals for the tape player to be turned off, walks to the front of the stage, and shouts at HOSEYN*]: Turn off

THE REX CINEMA TRIAL   131

that noise! [*Silence.*] "Woe be to him who finds fault and ridicules!"[24] [*Pause.*] "We have not come hither for ambition and glory; / We have come hither to take refuge from ill fate."[25] [*Addressing the audience*] We have come to take refuge with you. You are the purpose. You are the Mecca. You are the idols. I am nobody. [*Pointing to ALISHAHI*] He is nobody. Those who count are you, the people. Here, we are only the instruments and conduits. We are not the principal ones. The principal one is you. You. You. You must come here in my place and interrogate the murderer of your dear ones and avenge them. Of course, you might also be the target of insults. So be it. That is the way it goes. Truth is bitter, no matter who utters it. There is no difference between you and me. No matter whom you point to today, he will say that he is innocent. You cannot find anyone who is guilty anymore, God forbid. Everyone claims to be as infallible as the Twelve Imams and the Fourteen Infallible Ones.[26] [*Pause.*] Be careful. You made a revolution, and you must protect it. They will take this white bird away from you. If you are not careful, they will make it fly away! You must be alert. It will take time before this country becomes a sift and the rubbish is sifted out. It will take patience. Well, be patient. The hypocrite is sitting next to you. Let him. The opponent is talking sarcastically. Let him talk. Be patient. Don't get involved with him. Just keep an eye on him, so that he does not grab you by the throat. Make sure that he does not pull a weapon out of his pocket. But, as long as he is merely complaining, don't bother with him. Let him complain! Next defendant!

[*The COLONEL stands up and walks to the stage with dignity. The DIRECTOR's camera follows him.*]

Act II
Scene Three

ALISHAHI: What is your faith?

COLONEL: I am a Shi'ite, a Shi'ite Moslem.

ALISHAHI [*pointing to the book on the JUDGE's desk*]: Swear that you will tell the truth in response to all questions.

COLONEL: "I shall tell naught but what is right, / For crooked speech does not bring light."[27]

JA'FARI: Take a simple oath, without rhythm and rhyme.

COLONEL [*places his hand on the book*]: I swear that I shall utter naught but the truth.

JA'FARI: Please go there. [*The COLONEL walks to the defendant's stand.*] Identify yourself.

COLONEL: I request of the honorable court that I be allowed to say a few words before identifying myself.

JA'FARI [*after looking at ALISHAHI*]: Go ahead.

COLONEL: I am grateful. [*Pause.*] I did not make a revolution. I had no part in the revolution, because a soldier, in keeping with his duty and his oath as a soldier, has no right to interfere in political quarrels. And a revolution is a great political and social quarrel. Since in this great quarrel the main determining role belongs to the people, it must be respected. And since every revolution is an unorganized people's government, it must be admitted that mistakes will take place here and there and the individual rights of some people will be unjustly violated. Revolution is the great right of dissatisfied societies, and the rights of individuals in them are like a drop in a tumultuous sea. With these prefatory remarks, I do not expect to be befriended. On the contrary, I want to make the point that no matter what judgment is made in this court about me, even if it is unjust and unfair, I will consider it right and just, because I respect revolution as a great public right. Colonel Siyavash

Amini Al-e Aqa, son of Enayatollah, specialized in anti-terrorist operations, at your service.

JA'FARI: What is your connection with the Rex Cinema tragedy? Explain briefly.

COLONEL: I was given a special assignment to determine the cause of and prepare a report on the fire. I visited the scene of the incident and wrote a report of my findings, of which you have a copy.

JA'FARI: What did you determine was the cause of the accident?

COLONEL: The fire was set intentionally. It was so obvious that a local Fire Department official could have made the same determination.

JA'FARI: But they sent an anti-terrorist specialist, a high-ranking military official. Why? In order to whitewash the case in the interest of the regime, an experienced specialist was needed.

COLONEL: May I ask what has been whitewashed in my report, of which you have a copy?

ALISHAHI: We will get to that, too. First, can you explain, as an expert and not as a layman, how you proved that the fire was set intentionally?

COLONEL: Yes. May I use the floor plan?

ALISHAHI: Of course.

COLONEL [*begins to indicate the location of the Rex Cinema on the floor plan*]: The Rex Cinema was located on the second floor of a shopping mall. In fact, one of the first-floor stores was turned into the entrance to the cinema, which had steps leading to the second floor, then to an L-shaped hall. At the entrance, that is, downstairs, the ticket office and a small snack bar were located. Three doors opened to the auditorium from the side and two from the back. And here were the restrooms. Well, now, you can see that if the fire had been unintentional, it would have started from inside the auditorium, from one of the seats, from a match or a lighter used to light up a cigarette. In that case, it would have taken some time for the fire to gain strength, turn into flames, and spread to other areas. But the point is, the fire began at several points simultaneously. The points where the fire started were at all the doors that opened to the hallway. Why? Because, as you know, the point where

THE REX CINEMA TRIAL   135

a fire begins burns more intensely than other areas. This type of burning is mostly found in these areas. And why do I think that they were started simultaneously? Because the severity of the burning in these areas is about the same. It is clear that the arsonists—definitely more than one—set fire to the entrance doors to the auditorium simultaneously, with a very flammable fuel, such as gasoline or thinner, and then they walked down the stairs and escaped from the large entrance door to the theater. I said from the hallway, since if they had done this from inside the auditorium, naturally, people would have seen it. But in the hallway, there were no officials or anything to stop them.

[*Pause.*]

ALISHAHI: And then?

COLONEL [*stares at him and the floor plans for a while, stunned, as if preoccupied*]: Then? [*Pause.*] Well, the people burned, sir. People . . . burned . . . in fire. Men and women suddenly realize that fire is flaming into the theater from above these doors. Only a few people, including a woman by the name of Shahnaz Qanbari, if I am not mistaken, who were sitting near one of the doors, jumped through the fire into the hall and escaped with their lives. The rest, that is, the first row, seeing the fire, probably rush to escape, screaming. Where do they escape? Since there is fire pouring in from these doors, they rush towards the two relatively small exit doors located on either side of the screen. The seats are the greatest obstacle to their escape. The weaker ones, women and children, fall and are trampled underfoot. Because of the high flammability of the gasoline and its spreading to the insulation sheets inside the walls, within a few minutes a thick toxic smoke fills the auditorium. Here, probably as a result of the burning of the electrical wires, the lights also go out. Many do not even get the chance to move towards the exit doors, and right where they are on the seats, they suffocate. Some of them are found later embracing each other on the seats. The first row of young people, and those who were more agile and had reached the exit doors—here—begin to climb on each other's heads, but, unfortunately, the doors do not open.

JA'FARI: Those bastards had chained the doors from the outside.

COLONEL: No. These doors, rather than opening from inside to the outside, opened from the outside to the inside. Here, their own rushing to the doors and the pressure of their bodies prevented the doors from opening towards the inside. As a result, they, too, fell on each other, right here, and suffocated. [*Pause.*] The only luck that people had—if you could call it luck—was that before the fire reached their bodies, they suffocated. And they can thank God for this luck!

JA'FARI: Undoubtedly! It is obligatory for every living being to thank and praise The Most Compassionate and Merciful. Painful punishment still remains. You have no idea. The fire of Hell, it is said, has no smoke. It burns the skin and the flesh, but you do not die to be done with it. The burning continues.

COLONEL: I see.

JA'FARI: So, "Fear the fire whose fuel is the people, and stones which are prepared for the infidels."[28]

ALISHAHI: Alimohammadi, the Custodian of the Esfahani Mosque, has testified here that: "At the fire, the two entrance and exit doors of the theater were chained from the outside. I tried to hit it with the Blazer, but it did not open."

HOSEYN: Alimohammadi had no Blazer up his ass at that time. He drove a beat-up Peykan, which belonged to a relative of his wife, who had gone to Ahvaz.[29]

LIEUTENANT: Alimohammadi bought his Blazer two or three months afterwards. And now he probably rides in a bullet-proof Mercedes Benz.

JA'FARI: Continue!

COLONEL: I found no evidence of the entrance or exit doors being closed with a chain or anything else. A man had taken his child to the restroom before the fire started, and when he came back he saw that the doors to the auditorium were burning. He escaped by way of the stairs and exited from the large entrance door. Therefore, the doors were not closed from the outside. Qorban Palangi, the janitor of the cinema, and another young worker, whose name I do not remember, had gone to buy a sandwich or something. They returned at this time. Naturally, they entered through the same door. When they saw the smoke and fire, they took the fire extinguishers in the hallway to put out the fire. Unfortunately, they did not know how to operate them.

JA'FARI: Amazing. These two get a growl in their stomachs just before the fire and go to buy sandwiches.

THE REX CINEMA TRIAL 137

COLONEL: Even if they had not, they usually spent their time downstairs around the entrance and could not have prevented the fire. And supposing that they could have gotten to the second floor sooner. Still, since they did not know how to work the fire extinguishers, they could not do anything.

ALISHAHI: Your entire report is based on the theory that the doors to the auditorium were the points where the fire started. What about the inside the auditorium? Did you not identify other sources of fire inside the auditorium, such as flammable and explosive materials, toxic gas capsules, and so on?

COLONEL: No.

JA'FARI: There is evidence available that flammable materials and toxic gases used by Israel to destroy the residences of the Palestinian refugees and Moslems in Jerusalem were also used in the Rex Cinema. Since you are an expert in the identification and uncovering of terrorist acts, how is it that you did not find them?

COLONEL: I do not know anything about the evidence you have. You should show this evidence so that everyone, including me, can learn about it.

JA'FARI: People who, unlike you, do not claim to be experts on terrorism know about it.

ALISHAHI: On the floor of the auditorium, didn't you see anything to support this evidence?

COLONEL: If I had, I would have reported it.

ALISHAHI: Then, what did you see?

COLONEL: The things that I wrote down. Some half-burned men's, women's, and children's shoes. Two bottles of Pepsi and an empty can.

ALISHAHI: Couldn't the can have contained toxic gas?

COLONEL: Not the can I saw. It was a peanut can, the kind which can be found in the nut shop near the cinema. It was even clear that it had been purchased from that store.

ALISHAHI: Do you expect us to accept that the cause of the rapid suffocation of so many people was only the toxic gas emitted from insulation?

[*The COLONEL sorrowfully nods and snickers.*]

JA'FARI: What are you laughing about? Is the burning of so many Moslem men, women, and children, to which you confessed yourself, a laughing matter?

COLONEL: Don't be upset. I am not laughing at you. I am laughing at my own report. You convicted the previous defendant on the basis of this report. If you consider the previous defendant to be a party to the crime, that means that you have accepted the validity of the report. But, now, to convict me, you are trying to discredit it. I am laughing at my own report, which can be valid to convict one person and invalid to convict the next.

JA'FARI: Indeed, the report that you prepared is laughable!

ALISHAHI: What do you know about Alireza Ashurpur?

COLONEL: I did not mention anyone by name in my report, including this person, as a perpetrator of this fire.

ALISHAHI: I asked what you know.

COLONEL: Ashurpur was an arms smuggler and had a police record in Abadan. I saw his file. He smuggled weapons through Iraq and sold them to the opponents of the government. He was a boastful and talkative man. After the Rex Cinema incident, because he saw support for a religious revolution in the border towns of Iraq, he claimed there that he had had a hand in the Rex Cinema fire. And since the Iraqi government had good relations with the Shah's regime at the time, it delivered him to the Iranian border officials.

ALISHAHI: Then, Ashurpur did not have a hand in this incident?

COLONEL: No.

ALISHAHI: But he was identified as the one guilty of the Rex Cinema fire by the regime.

COLONEL: Yes.

ALISHAHI: And you knew that he was not guilty?

COLONEL: Correct.

ALISHAHI: But you did not say anything.

COLONEL: It was not my duty.

JA'FARI: How about your conscience? Did you not have a conscience? Then, what about the expertise for which you used to get a salary and benefits from this poor nation? Everywhere that I preached, I said that Ashurpur was innocent, that by identifying innocent people as the perpetrators, the Shah's regime was trying to cover up its own crimes. You were paid a salary as an anti-terrorist operations expert, and we risked our lives by telling the truth.

COLONEL: Look, I am not criticizing you for using every issue to discredit and dishonor the previous regime. What is astonishing to me is why you bring up the Ashurpur matter. They did not do anything to him anyway. They hastily announced his name in order to calm the anger of the public, who hungered for news of the arrest of the perpetrator or perpetrators of this crime. It is astonishing that you have more solid evidence against the previous regime, but you do not mention it. After the Ashurpur matter, one of the main perpetrators of the Rex Cinema incident was arrested. This perpetrator not only confessed to his crime but even revealed the names of the principal planners of the fire and those who worked with him. Rather than putting this person on trial in Abadan and bringing to trial the rest of his fellow criminals, who were known both to the people of Abadan and to the survivors of the martyrs of the Rex Cinema, they sent him and his file to Tehran to the Royal Guard. This is the evidence that exposes the regime. Rather than sending the criminal to the judicial authorities, he is sent to the Royal Guard.

HOSEYN: It was me, Colonel, Hoseyn Takbe'alizadeh. They sent me to the Guards.

JA'FARI: From the audience, please do not address the defendant.

HOSEYN: I am not one of the audience. I am helping out with the electricity; I am assisting the Director.

JA'FARI: Be quiet, sir. Do not do anything that will require me to request the help of the law enforcement officials to maintain order in the court.

[*To the COLONEL*] There is nothing new in that the tyrant's regime did not distinguish between the guilty and the innocent. It arrested everyone. It tortured everyone. Right now, if the people present here were asked how many of them had been jailed innocently and tortured during the past regime, many would raise their hands. This person who now claims to have been arrested and sent to the Guards is standing right before you here, which proves the confusion of the previous regime. Otherwise, if he were really guilty, would he be alive now? Would it have been any problem for them to kill a nobody like him?

COLONEL: The reason that the criminal was not put on trial and even his name was not announced was that the intelligence minister of the time had asked the Shah not to do it. In his initial confession, the criminal had revealed the names of persons who were members of a religious group and were among the students and followers of the Leader of the Revolution.[30] At that time, a meeting was to take place between General Katuzian and the Leader of the Revolution in Paris, so that the matter would be resolved peacefully. The intelligence minister of the time believed that announcing the names of the main perpetrators would destroy any chance for this meeting and its likely results. Furthermore, given the favorable attitude towards the religious groups at the time, the people would not have believed this one, as they had not believed the Ashurpur matter. Hence, the case was placed in the hands of the intelligence minister. The events following the Rex Cinema incident occurred so rapidly that there was no longer any opportunity to deal with this case. The files were lost in the early months of the revolution and the intelligence minister, who was only guilty of knowing about the case, was executed.

JA'FARI: You don't need to sing elegies for the enemies of the Revolution who were annihilated in accordance with the opinion of the Revolutionary Council and the order of the Leader of the Revolution.

COLONEL: Singing elegies is not my profession, my dear sir. Many know that the minister, Dr. Ameli-Tehrani, who was executed, was a noble, patriotic man of faith. He had been a critic and opponent of the previous regime for years. Even though he had been offered ministerial and parliamentary positions many times, he accepted a position only when he thought that the country was on the verge of collapse and that people like him should do something. You know yourself that he was a victim of the Rex Cinema incident and the identification of the perpetrators of the fire.

THE REX CINEMA TRIAL 141

ALISHAHI: Of the defendants, you are the only one who voluntarily contacted us and told us that you were prepared to take part in the trial in order to clarify the issues behind the scenes of the Rex Cinema tragedy. Why?

COLONEL: To say what I have been saying. Because, as an Iranian, I feel a sense of responsibility towards the families and relatives of the Rex Cinema martyrs.

JA'FARI: They were not martyrs. A martyr is a person who gives his life for truth, not the one who goes to see a nonsensical movie. [*To the DIRECTOR*] Now, I hope you are not offended!

ALISHAHI: We thought that you intended to reveal secrets that at the time, as an officer, you could not speak about, because of the expediencies of your job.

COLONEL: Certain points which have proven to be true with the passage of time were the only rumors at that time. But I tried not to let such rumors affect my report. I tried to stay within the framework of my actual observations and not to refer to issues for which I had no conclusive evidence.

ALISHAHI: For example?

COLONEL: For example, the likelihood of the involvement of religious extremists in the fire.

ALISHAHI: This was nothing to be afraid of. If you had written it down, the regime would have been very pleased and would probably have given you a bonus.

COLONEL: You might not believe it now, but at that time, I was also secretly sympathetic to the revolution.

JA'FARI: So, by hiding your secret thoughts, you in fact betrayed your benefactor. When you betray your own regime, what are you planning to do to a regime that is your enemy?

ALISHAHI: I have no more questions for this gentleman.

JA'FARI: By using his expertise in anti-terrorist operations, he tells us things today that he should have said a year ago, when the power was in the hands of his master. My last question to him is whether he made use of his expertise in the same manner in his other anti-terrorist assignments?

COLONEL: I will not answer this question.

JA'FARI: You have no answer to give, because more of your stinking actions will be revealed. You know that the regime used your anti-terrorist reports in suppressing the Islamic movement in Qom, Tabriz, Esfahan, and other places, and in killing and eradicating seminary students and clerics.

COLONEL: I will not answer, because this is a session to investigate the Rex Cinema incident. You are neither sufficiently qualified nor morally competent, nor do you have the reasoning, conscience, knowledge, or expertise to investigate the matter at hand—which is no insignificant matter. What are you talking about? A person who does not know how to ride should at least hold on to the saddle horn. [*Pause. The COLONEL stands up and walks confidently towards where the other defendants have been taken. But halfway, he turns back and once again begins.*] Why don't you take advantage of this golden opportunity that has come your way? Why don't you tell the people the truth and, in doing so, save your revolution that is so soon about to collapse? This trial is as important for the survival of the revolution as was the Rex Cinema incident for its success. Without this incident, Abadan might not have joined the rebellion. The oil industry would not have stopped operating, and the main artery of the regime would not have been severed. It is true that with the Rex Cinema tragedy, the religious fanatics caused the violent deaths of 400 innocent human beings; but, in exchange, they brought their revolution to victory. Just by explaining this truth to the people, you could remove this infectious, cancerous tumor from the body of the revolution forever. By identifying the main perpetrators, you could save the revolution from certain staining. You could even exonerate the planners and the main perpetrators of the fire, who are probably your friends, by explaining that they had no intention of killing anyone and engaged in this act only to bring the revolution to victory and make the people rebel against the regime. You could make the nation, which is still intoxicated with the victory of the revolution, forgive them. Unfortunately, you have not realized the value of this golden opportunity and once again took away from the people of this country, who have suffered for hundreds of years, the chance of bringing the revolution to victory.

[*The lights of the auditorium and the stage suddenly go off.*]

DIRECTOR: Battery, battery! Connect it to the battery!

[*HOSEYN's spotlight is turned on after some delay and lights up the stage. In the darkness of the stage, the COLONEL, who is being dragged out by two GUARDS, still continues.*]

COLONEL: With this action, you have proven that the "previous corrupt regime," as you call it, has been replaced by a bunch of hypocritical, lying charlatans who use the same methods as the previous regime to cover up their faults and corruption. By hiding the main criminals and convicting us, you will make heroes of ordinary and perhaps guilty people like us. In this shameless game, you are the losers, not us. . . .

[*The COLONEL is taken off the stage. Silence and darkness.*]

Act II
Scene Four

When the stage lights come on, the MANAGER OF THE THEATER is sitting at the defendant's stand. He is about 40 years old.

MANAGER OF THE THEATER: I am an employee of the Oil Industries. Managing the cinema is not my main job. First, I was an usher. I ushered people to their seats with a flashlight. Then I became a ticket taker at the door. And for a while, I operated the projector. After many years, the owner of the cinema had developed so much confidence in me that I was put in charge of the entire theater. I became the manager of the theater.

ALISHAHI: In that case, how did you manage to attend to your main job? If necessary, which job would you have sacrificed for the other?

MANAGER OF THE THEATER: Normally neither. The show times at the cinema, except for the holidays, were in the afternoon. And I worked only until 2 o'clock at the office.

ALISHAHI: Are you married?

MANAGER OF THE THEATER: Yes.

JA'FARI: How many dependents do you have?

MANAGER OF THE THEATER: My wife, two children, and my mother, who lives with us.

JA'FARI: When did you spend time with your wife and children? You didn't have any time. Did you?

MANAGER OF THE THEATER: I am ashamed. I am ashamed in the face of my wife and my children. I know I was never a good father. During all these years we never took a trip together. If there was a holiday, during which time they rarely went anywhere, I was not with them. Whenever my wife leafed through the family picture album, she said that I was missing from all the pictures.

ALISHAHI: Where were you on the night of the incident?

MANAGER OF THE THEATER: At 9 o'clock I took over the ticket office. The cashier turned over the account for the last show and left. Three hundred and eighty-seven tickets had been sold. I recorded the sales for that day in the books, left some cash in the box, and took the rest to deposit in the bank the next day. In the hallway, Qorban Palangi, the janitor, asked me if I wanted him to bring the car from the parking lot. I said no, I was going to get it myself. Qorban loved to drive, but he didn't have a license. Sometimes when he brought the car from the parking lot, he took a ride around the streets, and I was always worried that he might crash into a wall.

ALISHAHI: So, Qorban saw you in the hallway when you left the theater?

MANAGER OF THE THEATER: Yes. From the theater, I went directly home. As usual, the children had eaten their supper and mine was in the oven to stay warm. In the middle of my supper, Qorban called to say that.... [*Pause.*]

JA'FARI: Why did you not stay at the cinema until the film was over? Perhaps you had a vision that there was going to be danger.

MANAGER OF THE THEATER: For the last show, except for two or three people, the rest of the employees go home. All cinemas operate like that. I never stayed for the last show, unless I had a guest or something.

ALISHAHI: How many years have you worked in the theater?

MANAGER OF THE THEATER: Twenty-five years.

ALISHAHI: All this time with the Rex Cinema?

MANAGER OF THE THEATER: Twenty-one years at the Rex Cinema.

ALISHAHI: In the course of all these years, didn't you ever notice that the exit doors were installed backwards, that is, they opened towards the inside rather than the outside?

MANAGER OF THE THEATER: No, I always thought that was the way they were supposed to be.

ALISHAHI: You never had any problems?

THE REX CINEMA TRIAL 147

MANAGER OF THE THEATER: No. Perhaps it was because one of the workers would always open the exit door wide before the movie ended for the people to get out.

ALISHAHI: So, there was someone in charge of the exit door too?

MANAGER OF THE THEATER: Yes.

ALISHAHI: But on the night of the incident it seems that he was not there.

MANAGER OF THE THEATER: Yes, unfortunately. That night he was in the auditorium too and burned with the rest. He slept in the theater at night. He had no family. No one came to his grave. Everybody's grave was visited on the third, seventh, and fortieth days after they were buried, but not his.

JA'FARI: Have you ever thought, if those damned doors had been installed properly or if you had taught your workers how to use the fire extinguishers, how many lives would have been saved?

MANAGER OF THE THEATER: Yes, I have. What can I say? I didn't know how to operate the fire extinguishers myself.

JA'FARI: Isn't that something? A man lives off the people who come to the theater for a lifetime and doesn't even think about their safety!

MANAGER OF THE THEATER: If you want to conclude that not knowing how to operate the fire extinguishers or the improper installation of the doors were my fault, okay, go right ahead. I don't intend to defend myself. To tell the truth, I don't—how can I say it—feel like going on living. Otherwise, I would have listened to my wife and left. She begged me not to stay. She said, eventually, when they can't get anyone else, they will come and arrest you. I said, where can I go anyway? Wherever I go, can I refuse to take my head with me? Can I stop talking? Can I go anywhere where, when I am eating, I won't see people jumping up and down in the fire?

JA'FARI: Well, this itself means you feel guilty, even if we don't call it confessing your guilt.

MANAGER OF THE THEATER: This is feeling miserable, not feeling guilty. You can say whatever you like, but I don't consider myself guilty. In terms of safety, the Rex Cinema was no better or worse than any other theaters. Go take a look. If this had happened in any other theater, the results would have been exactly the same. There would have been the same number of people in the theater and about the same number of casualties. If the doors were not installed properly, it is the fault of the City Hall that issued a permit for the building, and the Culture and Arts Office that reviewed and extended this permit every year, despite all the faults. If the other workers and I did not know how to work the fire extinguishers, that is because they are only for decoration, and the Security and Fire Department inspectors do not take their jobs seriously and do not care whether anyone can operate such equipment. If the one or two law enforcement agents who used to be on watch in every theater are no longer there, it is the fault of the Police Department, which rounded up all its agents to have them guard only the oil refinery. Now, should I pay compensation for all this mismanagement? I have no objection. But at least don't expect me to consider myself guilty. What I am saying here has nothing to do with my feeling guilty. It is because I sympathize with those who sent their brothers, sisters, or children to a cinema that I was in charge of, and then they had to come and take away their burned bodies. It is feeling sorry for Abolfazl, the worker in the cinema, or Naser, the projectionist. [*Pause.*]

ALISHAHI: Wasn't the projectionist also among the victims?

MANAGER OF THE THEATER [*sorrowfully*]: Yes. He was twenty years old. He was saving money to go abroad to study cinema. Any time we showed a bad movie, he would somehow let me know. He would say: "Mr. Dehqani, sit down and watch this movie; see what garbage we show the people. He was right. Sometimes the movie was so obscene and upsetting that I was ashamed to watch it with my family. I would say: Well, Naser, this is the kind of thing they are making here. You can't import Iranian movies from abroad. You go abroad, study, and come back to make better movies, and we will show them and be proud of you.

ALISHAHI: Besides the two that you mentioned, did you know of anyone else specifically among the victims? [*Pause.*]

MANAGER OF THE THEATER: Specifically! You would not believe it! Rahim Aqa, the lantern-maker, had brought his wife and two kids to see Aghasi's movie.[31] The kids were twins, two thirteen- or fourteen-year-old boys. The Aghasi movie was going to be the next feature. Rahim came to see me and said: "You were supposed to show the Aghasi movie this week." I said, "God willing, next week." He said: "So, how is this movie, 'Gavazn-ha'? Is it worth seeing?" I said: "It is a good movie; the people have liked it, so we held it over for one more week." He went and bought four tickets and came in.

JA'FARI [*to the DIRECTOR*]: You scored four more corpses, Mr. Director.

MANAGER OF THE THEATER: I was one hundred percent responsible for these four to come in. But did I have any idea what was going to happen?

JA'FARI: Don't you feel guilty, even for these four people? Even if you call it unintentional murder, still there are four of them.

MANAGER OF THE THEATER: I feel guilty about these four: Rahim, his wife, and his fourteen-year-old twins.

JA'FARI: The revolution has had many of these fourteen-year-old victims. Many of these young innocent people became the prey of the poisonous snakes of Zahhak.[32] It is said that no loss is as painful as the loss of young people; and the loss of no young person is as painful as the loss of the eleven-year-old Infallible One in Karbala.[33] [*Sings like professional religious mourners.*] His mother had dressed his beloved body in his new wedding clothes.

HOSEYN [*begins to mourn*]: "Little sparrow, poof, poof, poof. Don't sit on the edge of our roof."

JA'FARI [*continues to sing with the same tone*]: "The holy family was preparing his wedding chamber for him in the camp. He came to his revered uncle and asked permission to go to battle. He was only eleven. The Sire of the Martyrs said:[34] I will not permit you to go into battle because I cannot bear to see the suffering of your new bride. Qasem was very upset.[35] He could not look at the beloved face of his revered uncle. Shyness prevented him. . . ."

[*ALISHAHI turns on the tape player and weeping is heard from it.*]

HOSEYN: "You'll roll into the painted pond."

JA'FARI: "Softly, he said: Dearest Uncle! Tell my new bride not to worry. My death will not stop our union. It is union itself. Our wedding chamber has already been prepared at the side of the Kowsar Pond, before my grandfather the Prophet.[36] My grandfather is waiting for us."

[*Darkness. JA'FARI recites some unintelligible verses in the dark. The curtain falls. Only the song on HOSEYN's tape player is heard in the auditorium.*]

Act III
Scene One

The curtain opens. On the stage a guard takes LIEUTENANT BAHMANI to the defendant's stand.

LIEUTENANT: Don't touch me! Move aside!

ALISHAHI: Here, please. First take an oath.

LIEUTENANT: I swear by this book that you are lying. Is that sufficient?

JA'FARI: No. The oath must refer to you.

ALISHAHI: The defendant shows his position clearly by his oath.

LIEUTENANT: I swear on what I believe in. I believe that you yourselves are the perpetrators of the Rex Cinema crime.

JA'FARI: At least swear that you will tell the truth, so that the people will believe you.

LIEUTENANT: I swear by this book that you are from the lineage of the corruptors of the earth.[37] [*To ALISHAHI*] And you are from the lineage of the cronies who get anywhere only by pimping for the corruptors of the earth. [*The GUARD cocks his gun.*] Fire! Fire! Fire, if you so wish. Empty your rifle, you son-of-a-bitch. Do what you will do after this sham trial right now.

[*ALISHAHI sends the GUARD out.*]

JA'FARI: "Do not fight the ignorant," says the Koran. If we do as you do, we will be just like you: servants of the tyrant!

ALISHAHI: That is, the instruments of whipping and torture, violence, suffocation, and terrorism.

LIEUTENANT: Which you are not?

ALISHAHI: Whatever we are, at least we are different from you in that, despite all the insults from you, we will allow you to defend yourself. And not in the narrow, closed rooms of SAVAK, or in the damp, stinking basements of the Police Department, but in public, before television cameras.

LIEUTENANT: This proves your shamefulness, that without any fear of the people, you display your disgracefulness, even on television.

[*The LIEUTENANT goes to the defendant's stand. Silence.*]

ALISHAHI [*reads off a note*]: First name, Manuchehr; last name, Bahmani; son of Yusof; born in Amol; occupation, police officer in Khuzestan; rank, first lieutenant; place of service, Abadan Police Department. Do you verify this information?

[*Silence.*]

JA'FARI: What is it? Is he pretending to be deaf, or does he need to be coaxed?

ALISHAHI: If you have a question, please go ahead. Silence indicates consent.

JA'FARI: But he is the kind that might even say that his name was not said correctly.

LIEUTENANT: What kind of ridiculous game is this, anyway? Have you not already determined that I am guilty?

JA'FARI: It is clear to us that you are. I want it to become clear to the people. The purpose of these questions and answers is to make the facts known to them.

LIEUTENANT: Well, why should I not ask you questions? This way the truth might become more clear. And I am sure it will.

JA'FARI: You ask questions?

LIEUTENANT: Why not?

JA'FARI: This is something new.

ALISHAHI: Where have you seen the law that says the defendant puts the judge on trial?

THE REX CINEMA TRIAL 153

LIEUTENANT: Is this a trial? Are you talking to me about law? On the basis of what laws is this court operating?

ALISHAHI: On the basis of revolutionary trials.

LIEUTENANT: If it is on the basis of revolutionary trials, that means that anything goes. Well, why shouldn't I ask you questions?

ALISHAHI: You are a defendant!

LIEUTENANT: You are being kind! I am guilty. Didn't the judge just say so? My guilt is proven to you! Didn't he say that these questions and answers are only to clarify the truth? I promise you that if I ask the questions, the truth will become clearer.

JA'FARI: You mean, we shouldn't ask you any questions at all?

LIEUTENANT: Yes. But first I will ask a few questions. Then I will be at your disposal.

JA'FARI: Well, let him ask questions, sir.

ALISHAHI: But, Haj Aqa. . . .

JA'FARI: Let him ask. It is said, "He who has nothing to hide has no fear of being searched." Ask, sir! Ask whatever you wish!

LIEUTENANT: In the preliminary investigations, I gave you a few names as the main planners of the Rex Cinema fire. Why are none of them present in this court of injustice?

ALISHAHI: You were asked if you knew anyone in the Police Department or SAVAK who was involved in this incident. You could reveal their names for a reduction in your sentence. Instead, you mentioned the names of people who are all respectable and opposed to the previous regime. You might just as well have accused the entire Iranian nation of this act. Should we have summoned them to the court?

LIEUTENANT: I only gave you five names whom the people in Abadan know especially well. Suppose I were slandering them; shouldn't they have been summoned so they could clear their names? Maybe the consciences of some of them would have been awakened at seeing so many waiting victims, and they would have confessed. Are people like Rashidian and Kiavosh now so prominent that they cannot be summoned to the court?

JA'FARI: In fact, I contacted Messrs. Rashidian and Kiavosh by telephone. Both denied any connection with the Rex Cinema tragedy.

HOSEYN: Isn't that something!

LIEUTENANT: Why didn't they come to the court to deny it?

JA'FARI: What expectations you have! Did you expect the representative of the Islamic Consultative Assembly, with his busy schedule and all his responsibilities, to come to Abadan from Tehran because you wanted him to?

LIEUTENANT: Were these two anything more than a couple of rickety school teachers of religion up to a few months ago? Since you have rewarded one of them with the job of representative of Ahvaz and the other one that of the representative of Abadan, what is there that people like these can do in that infested Parliament which is more important than investigating this tragedy, something that so many of the people of Khuzestan have been hurt by and are sensitive about? Aren't these two so-called representatives representing these people? Or that beggar bum you put in the Guards Corps?

HOSEYN: Yeah, him. Tell them about him.

JA'FARI: Please avoid mentioning the names of others not connected with this court, and especially calling people offensive and insulting names!

LIEUTENANT: Supposing that those two are far away or, as you say, engaged in sensitive occupations. Ali Mohammadi, the custodian of the Esfahani Mosque, is very close to you. This man, while the fire was still burning and before the Fire Department got there, had spread the rumor in the city that government agents had set the Rex Cinema on fire. The Esfahani Mosque is a long way away from the Rex Cinema. Doesn't this in itself prove that he knew about it, or that the people who set the Rex Cinema on fire had contacted him by telephone and told him? Or, where is Abolpur, the Petroleum college student whom you appointed as the director of education? The Department of Education is very close to here. The whole city knows that he was awarded the position for his participation in this very conspiracy.

JA'FARI: Both persons that you mentioned were summoned in the preliminary interrogations. The minutes are here. Both swore on the Koran before witnesses that they had no connection with the Rex Cinema incident.

HOSEYN: May the Koran strike them dead.

LIEUTENANT: How about the Friday Imam of Abadan, Hojjat al-Islam Jami, who is the instigator of all these problems? How about him? Did he also swear that he has done nothing?

JA'FARI: The rumors about the Friday Imam were spread by a woman by the name of Naneh Namaki, who sang religious elegies in women's gatherings without permission. We summoned this woman. She confessed before witnesses that she had made up this statement out of personal animosity.

HOSEYN: First it was leaked by Karim's mother. There were four of us. We were supposed to get forty. Karim got sick on the way and vomited. Like he had been poisoned. We were forced to leave him and go. When the job was done, he came asking for his share of ten. Well, what for? He hadn't come with us. We had a quarrel, and he went and told his mother. . . .

JA'FARI: Hey, sir, sir . . . after all, this is a court. Now he has started to tell stories!

LIEUTENANT: Is this not a court of the revolution-stricken people? Let the people talk. Poor thing!

JA'FARI: Let him. Everyone can talk, but not at the same time. Let us finish with you, then anyone who wants to can come and talk. In fact, we have asked them to talk.

ALISHAHI: Lieutenant, if Your Honor's questions are finished, maybe we can impose on you for a couple of questions!

LIEUTENANT: One more question.

ALISHAHI: Please.

LIEUTENANT: After the fire, the Police Department Officers were given special assignments to find and arrest suspicious individuals. Specific instructions were given to keep an eye on those individuals who were trying to blame the government for this tragedy and who intended to start disturbances. One of those suspicious individuals who called the people to riot was you, yourself. Correct?

JA'FARI: You are using the word "suspicious" improperly. I openly called the people to riot. The regime was trying to blame the opposition, especially the religious groups, for this crime. From the pulpit, with proof and evidence, I proved to the people that this was the government's doing and asked them to take revenge against the murderers of their dear ones. Yes, these things were said that led to your being where you are today, and our being where we are! I wasn't afraid of anyone. At that time, I was ready to risk my life, and I still am.

LIEUTENANT: The night that you were returning from Farahabad Mosque, I was chasing you. . . .

JA'FARI: You should say the Qods Mosque. The name Farah can no longer be attached to holy places.[38] Those days are over.

LIEUTENANT: I was chasing you. You were riding on the back of a motorcycle and, in order not to be recognized, had taken off your turban and robe and placed them in a sack.

JA'FARI: I hadn't done so to avoid being recognized. The turban would have blown off.

LIEUTENANT: And the robe would also probably have blown off. I ordered you to stop several times. You continued on. It was obvious that you were speeding to escape.

JA'FARI: The motorcycle engine was loud. We couldn't hear your order.

LIEUTENANT: I stopped you. You insulted me, and I struck you on the face.

JA'FARI: I didn't insult you. I protested your turning in front of the motorcycle, like a barbarian. Both my companion, the offspring of the Prophet, and I were nearly killed.

LIEUTENANT: I struck you on the face, correct?

JA'FARI: Yes, you struck me, and hard, too. And you struck me twice.

THE REX CINEMA TRIAL

LIEUTENANT: And today, out of all those police officers who were pursuing suspicious persons and rioters, I am the only one who is being tried for participation in the Rex Cinema fire and will certainly be executed. [*Pause.*] I have no further questions.

[*Silence.*]

[*ALISHAHI and JA'FARI begin to talk together.*]

ALISHAHI: You go ahead.

JA'FARI: No, you go ahead, please.

ALISHAHI: Before I begin my main question, since you yourself confessed to having struck a cleric, I would ask you for a brief explanation. As a police officer, were you allowed to strike anyone?

LIEUTENANT: No, I was not. But, after all, a police officer, too, sometimes becomes angry, even makes mistakes.

ALISHAHI: Then you admit that you had no legal right to try and punish anyone right there and then?

LIEUTENANT: Yes, I had no legal right.

ALISHAHI: Then do not criticize us for not observing certain principles that you call law in this court. For years, thousands of violations of law were committed by government agents until they led to the revolution and, consequently, a trial such as this.

LIEUTENANT: I admit that what I did was wrong. But every wrong has a particular punishment. There is no reason why, for striking this gentleman, I should be identified as a perpetrator of the Rex Cinema crime and be punished for it.

ALISHAHI: We will get to that, too. For now, my main question: The Rex Cinema was located relatively close to the Police Station. Correct?

LIEUTENANT: Yes.

ALISHAHI: The Police Department, if only for the sake of its own security, should have been more watchful around that area, don't you think?

LIEUTENANT: Probably.

ALISHAHI: But no one was assigned around the theater.

LIEUTENANT: All the officers had been removed from the cinemas. It was not just the Rex Cinema.

ALISHAHI: Yes, the manager of the theater said the same thing. They had removed the officers from the cinemas and sent them somewhere else, somewhere where there was more profit to be gained.

LIEUTENANT: What does all this have to do with me? They had concentrated the forces in the refinery because the main objective was terrorist acts against the Oil Company. In fact, all this mess was to put the Oil Company out of operation, which it did. You know this better than I do.

ALISHAHI: But the officers were not only assigned to the Oil Company. Several were also assigned to the cabaret and the bar of the Persia Hotel. Correct? [*Pause.*] Precisely eight or nine people?

LIEUTENANT: Yes.

ALISHAHI: And you were one of them.

LIEUTENANT: I was ordered to. An officer does not choose his own assignments.

ALISHAHI: But that was not the Oil Company.

LIEUTENANT: It was a place where foreigners frequented and stayed.

ALISHAHI: Foreigners also stayed at and frequented other hotels. That was a place of debauchery.

LIEUTENANT: The Leader of the Revolution had ordered the cabarets and casinos to be bombed. . . .

JA'FARI: The Leader of the Revolution had not ordered any such thing. His decree was to avoid centers of corruption, that anyone who operates such centers and anyone who frequents such places is not one of us.

LIEUTENANT: In any case, as a result of that decree, these centers were constantly threatened by the religious groups.

ALISHAHI: In this city there were other cabarets and other centers of debauchery; but the Police Department had assigned guards only to the Persia Hotel. How long have you been living in Abadan?

LIEUTENANT: I grew up in Abadan.

ALISHAHI: Most men from Abadan know that there were more imports in terms of blondes of the gentler sex in this hotel and cabaret than in other places.

LIEUTENANT: Conclusion?

ALISHAHI: That this hotel was also a place of pleasure for the prominent people for when they came to the south on business, which, of course, was always the pretext.

LIEUTENANT: Conclusion?

ALISHAHI: That the executed general, the deputy chief of police of the country—who was executed some time ago—had particularly close ties with the owner of this hotel, and on every trip special souvenirs and first-rate imports were at his disposal. And for this reason, the Abadan Police Department had to guard that place.

LIEUTENANT: Supposing that was the case, how am I to blame? When I am assigned to guard a location can I say no?

ALISHAHI: Of course you can't. Especially when such an assignment is not without its pleasure and when it suits one's tastes and nature. After all, would a wise man of good taste leave blonde ladies to go protect thick oil pipes?

JA'FARI: God protect us.

LIEUTENANT: How is all this related to the Rex Cinema?

ALISHAHI: The relation is that the Police Department leaves all the centers of corruption and non-corruption, which, as you say, were threatened by the opposition, and sends guards to two places: the oil refinery and—pardon me—an unofficial whorehouse. For the regime, two centers needed to be protected: money and whores. And it was accidental that you served in the second center. That is, you were the doorman at the whorehouse. Then here I am accused, by you, of being a servant and a pimp. [*To JA'FARI.*] He is yours.

[*Silence.*]

JA'FARI: Before the cinema fire, you were not in Abadan. Correct?

LIEUTENANT: For my two weeks of annual vacation I had gone to Ahvaz.

JA'FARI: On what day did your vacation end? Do you remember?

LIEUTENANT: On the 29th of Mordad [*20 August*].

JA'FARI: Then, when did you return?

LIEUTENANT: On the 28th of Mordad [*19 August*].

JA'FARI: Why one day earlier?

LIEUTENANT: What's wrong with that?

JA'FARI: That was the day of the incident.

LIEUTENANT: What does that have to do with me? I came back to tend to my private affairs, do my house work, and get ready to go back to work the next day.

JA'FARI: Then why were you seen around the cinema at the time of the incident?

LIEUTENANT: I had come to help. I was home when this happened. My house is not too far from the cinema. I was told that the Rex Cinema was on fire. I immediately put on my clothes and went to help. Wouldn't you have done the same? Who am I asking!

JA'FARI: Who told you about it?

LIEUTENANT: The police supervisor, Mohammad Kari.

THE REX CINEMA TRIAL 161

JA'FARI: Aha! The one who is known as Naughty Mohammad. All the people in Abadan complain about him. A sly fox like you would have such a witness!

LIEUTENANT: Now you are talking nonsense. If we had had any hand in this, like you, we would have been hiding in some deep hole rather than coming and risking our lives to see if we might save some poor person from the fire. It wasn't only me. All the officers and police that had heard the news were also working hard. Our commander, Colonel Khonafar, was more involved than anyone else. On his orders, we tried to break down the side wall of the cinema by climbing the Fire Department ladders. If being present around the cinema is a crime, it has to be for all the officers and, more than everyone else, the commander of the operations, Colonel Khonafar, who is sitting with the defendants who will get at most two years of jail sentence. Is this your Islamic justice?

JA'FARI: I have nothing more to say to this person.

LIEUTENANT: You present yourselves as the supporters of the weak while your main talent lies in killing the weak. Your principal slogan is that the government, that is, SAVAK and the police, in order to disgrace the revolutionaries and promote the regime of the Shah, set fire to the Rex Cinema and that this was, in fact, planned by the Shah himself. Supposing that is the case. Then why did you let the main planner leave? Your leader insisted from the very beginning that he must leave. Now that he is gone, you say he must return?[39] If he was supposed to return, why did you first set the condition that he must leave, so that later you could kill some poor policeman, or a hard-working warrant officer, or someone like me, for being guilty of serving him? Is this not killing the weak?

JA'FARI: How long should we listen to the nonsensical talk of this man?

[*ALISHAHI rises. In order to have his voice better heard, he comes in front of the stage and, simultaneously with the LIEUTENANT, begins to talk.*]

ALISHAHI: Here we declare the end of the trial of the primary defendants. Before the examination of the secondary defendants, the court will take a recess.

LIEUTENANT: The Shah's greatest crime was that in regards to you clerics, he did not follow his father's policy and allowed you leeches to grow. And when the situation fell apart, he picked up his dogs and cats and left, throwing us to you wolves.

JA'FARI [*to offstage*]: Someone come here.

LIEUTENANT: And my crime is that that night, instead of striking you, I did not place a bullet in your skull.

JA'FARI: I will personally place the rope around your neck.

[*The LIEUTENANT suddenly attacks JA'FARI, grabs him by the collar, and pins him down on the desk.*]

ALISHAHI: Curtain! Curtain!

[*The curtain is closed, and the lights in the auditorium are turned on.*]

HOSEYN: Where are you going? Wait! Are the primary defendants finished? Then what about me? Gentlemen, don't go. Wait.

GUARD: It is the intermission.

HOSEYN: What do you mean, intermission? They are white-washing the whole affair. I was the one who set the Rex Cinema on fire. I thought that after the Lieutenant they would call me. At least say something. Where are you going? [*Goes on the stage and walks before the curtain.*] I am telling you, I myself went to the hallway and poured gasoline on the doors. Do I have to say it more clearly? What the Colonel said was right. It was airplane fuel. Abdollah Lorqaba, who was a member of the Airport Islamic Society, had brought it for us. We had poured it into cans and Pepsi bottles and put them in paper bags like they were pistachio nuts. In the middle of the movie Fallah said: "Now is the time; everybody is involved in the movie." Me and Farajollah Bazrkar were supposed to go and pour the gasoline at the bottom of the doors in the hallway, and he would be keeping watch from inside, so that as soon as he left, we would strike the match. We went to the hallway. Farajollah went from the back door and I from the side door. There was nobody in the hallway. I started immediately, took the can of gasoline out of the bag, and poured it at the bottom of all three doors. I couldn't see Farajollah but could hear the gasoline pouring in the back hallway. Someone came out of the back door. I thought it was Fallah. I struck the match.

JA'FARI [*angrily comes to the front stage, through the curtain*]: What is this show you are putting on? What have you got to say to the people? If you have something to say, tell me. You want to be put on trial? All right! I will try you.

Act III
Scene Two

JA'FARI: Open the curtain. [*The curtain opens. Again, lights are turned up on stage and down in the audience.*] Is there anyone else who wants to be tried? We have no objection. It is a friendly gathering. [*To ALISHAHI*] End the recess. We will try him. [*Takes HOSEYN towards the defendant's stand.*]

ALISHAHI [*in front of the stage*]: Friends. We have heard that generally some people take risks in either profitable enterprises or those that bring glory to them. But this friend of ours is doing this in order to place himself with the primary defendants. He probably thinks that they are giving something away for free in the first row. Well, in order to better prove to you, friends, how fair and flexible this revolutionary court is, we will give him the opportunity to try his luck, as the saying goes. So much the better. "The best is in whatever will happen."[40] If this will help clarify the behind-the-scenes events of the Rex Cinema tragedy, why not?

[*During ALISHAHI's speech, the DIRECTOR tries to show on television a picture of JA'FARI, who is speaking to HOSEYN at the back of the stage. With one hand, he holds the book in front of HOSEYN; with his other hand, he makes threatening gestures. HOSEYN nods obediently.*]

HOSEYN: Alright. I said alright.

JA'FARI: Well, go. Go say whatever is in your aching heart.

HOSEYN [*behind the podium*]: I, Hoseyn Takbe'alizadeh. . . . [*Pause, as if he is frightened.*]

JA'FARI: Father?

HOSEYN: I have none.

JA'FARI: Mother?

HOSEYN: Zahra.

JA'FARI: Occupation?

HOSEYN: None.

JA'FARI: How do you make a living?

HOSEYN: What?

JA'FARI: Where do you get money to eat?

HOSEYN: Well, sometimes I did some business, and sometimes I got pocket money from my mother.

JA'FARI: How did your mother make money?

HOSEYN: My mother is a shopkeeper. Around Ahmadabad.

JA'FARI: What kind of shop?

HOSEYN: Sells sandwiches.

[*Pause.*]

JA'FARI: Only sandwiches?

HOSEYN: Well, she has drinks, too.

JA'FARI: You said you occasionally did some business. What business?

HOSEYN: Before, I made money any way I could. But since I was guided to the right path, I repented. I stopped doing certain things. I used to sell cassette tapes, religious mourning tapes. Later on, only the speeches of His Reverence.[41] I made a living somehow or other.

JA'FARI: How about from SAVAK? Did you receive anything from SAVAK?

[*Silence.*]

HOSEYN [*upset*]: No fair!

JA'FARI: Then, how do you claim to have set fire to the Rex Cinema? Free of charge? SAVAK probably paid you. Remember, you are under oath.

HOSEYN: Sir, did I even know SAVAK, to have received money from. . . ?

JA'FARI: Maybe you didn't. But those others that you hung around with and worked with had received money from SAVAK. And they gave you some of it.

HOSEYN: You mean Haj Aqa Khorrami and the Friday Imam, both. . . .

JA'FARI: Why are you talking nonsense, boy? Those two who set fire to the cinema with you. I am talking about those two. You have taken an oath!

HOSEYN: But I told you, the two were Farajollah Bazrkar and Fallah.

JA'FARI: Well, maybe those two received money from SAVAK. You wouldn't know.

HOSEYN: Don't say this, sir. It won't please God to speak ill of a dead man. . . . Poor Fallah gave his life for this. You want more? The only thing that Farajollah had was a small shop in the Safa Bazaar in Jamshidabad. He repaired radios and things like that. Two days after the Rex Cinema incident, the Safa Bazaar in Jamshidabad went up in flames. Don't you remember? This Farajollah set his own store on fire to escalate the riots. The fire spread from there to the bazaar. And from then on, nobody saw Farajollah. Now, he is lost, and Fallah was burned with the people in the Rex Cinema. Is this their reward, to say that they were working for SAVAK?

JA'FARI: Are you supposed to defend yourself or them?

HOSEYN: Do you think I would have worked with them if they had been working with SAVAK?

JA'FARI: Well, you didn't know. God Almighty!

HOSEYN: I didn't know and neither did Haj Aqa Khorrami? They were his protégés. The Friday Imam didn't know either? And you didn't know either? Forgive me, but whenever I came to listen to you preach, you were even friendlier to Farajollah than to me.

JA'FARI: This is no proof! Abujahl, too, sat and listened to the Prophet preach, and misunderstood everything that the Messenger of God said.[42]

HOSEYN: These people were real devotees. Even if they are not here, their God is. The struggle that the four of us were involved in, nobody could dream of. Yadollah is alive; ask him. How many times do you think we used needles and razors to prick and cut the legs of girls who wore no stockings or wore miniskirts? How many prostitutes do you think we did in the Dub red-light district? Did we get a red cent for all of this from anyone? We did it for God. Only when we set fire to the pig pen of Khosrowabad did Haji give us something.

ALISHAHI: Sir, these things don't really have anything to do with the subject of the Rex Cinema.

HOSEYN: I am giving our background, Mr. Alishahi. If we hadn't had a good background, they wouldn't have asked us to do other things ... pouring kerosene on 250 pigs and setting them on fire isn't easy. This was our background when we came to the meetings; the meetings at the Qods Mosque, meetings at the home of. . . .

JA'FARI: Have you taken an oath, boy, to talk only about yourself and those other two dead ones? Why are you jumping about from subject to subject?

HOSEYN: May I give my life for your holy ancestor. You are slandering me. I, too. . . .

JA'FARI [*helplessly*]: I don't understand what he is talking about.

HOSEYN: Sir, what language do you think I'm speaking?

ALISHAHI: Let us handle it another way. Look, my friend, one of you three was killed in the fire, as you say.

HOSEYN: Fallah.

ALISHAHI: And another, as you confess, had a hand in the fire of the Safa Bazaar in Jamshidabad, who has also disappeared.

HOSEYN: Farajollah.

ALISHAHI: Well, didn't you ever ask yourself why he has disappeared? Would an adult just disappear for no reason? Use your head a bit. Maybe he knew all the secrets. Maybe SAVAK did him in to destroy the evidence. . . . No, don't talk! Just listen. If, as you say, he set fire to his own shop for the revolution, should he have disappeared instead of coming here with his head high and proudly demanding his reward from the revolution?

THE REX CINEMA TRIAL 169

JA'FARI: Obviously, there was something secretive about him. We looked everywhere you could imagine for him, didn't we?

ALISHAHI: Yes, we did! We looked for him because of the bazaar fire, because from one end of the Jamshidabad Safa Bazaar to the other were shops of poor tradesmen. He destroyed everything these poor folks had, which is not a revolutionary action. Revolution means to fight imposed force, to fight imperialism. His Honor is taking your side in saying that perhaps those two knew that they were the agents of the dirty plans of SAVAK and that you cooperated with them unwittingly.

HOSEYN: How about Mirsofyani? [*To JA'FARI*] Excuse me, but I can't keep from saying anything about this one. Mirsofyani was the one who gave us the money. He said it was from Haji. He didn't say it was from SAVAK. He said the money was from Haji, the one who now heads the strike force. Why don't you summon him?

ALISHAHI: You are right!

JA'FARI: That mouth must be. . . .

ALISHAHI: He is right! I have a report about that individual here. [*He looks for it among the files.*] A report verified personally by Hajjat al-Islam Jami, the Friday Imam of Abadan. This person was in the SAVAK jail for a while and was probably released for promising cooperation. He was a student of Mr. Rashidian, a faithful and intelligent student, who frequented the meetings at the home of the Friday Imam to learn and be guided.

JA'FARI: Everybody did it. The home of a prayer leader is not like that of a king, where guards stand watch. Anyone who wishes comes in and anyone who wishes leaves. No one can stop anyone.

ALISHAHI: In these meetings, he notices that some of the devotees of the Islamic Revolution ask His Reverence's permission to set fire to banks and government establishments as an expression of opposition to the regime.

JA'FARI: Obviously. No one denies this struggle. Of the 420 movie theaters in the country, 119 were set on fire: 32 in Tehran and 87 in the provincial cities. But did anybody even get a scratch in those theaters?

ALISHAHI: Finally, under the pressure of the revolutionaries, the Friday Imam agrees, provided the locations chosen are among the centers of corruption or belong to the Tyrant himself, and that the lives and property of the downtrodden Moslem people are by no means put in jeopardy. The person that you named reports the matter to SAVAK, which plays a trick, as they say, and sets the Rex Cinema, full of people, on fire in order to create public hatred of the revolution and the revolutionaries.

JA'FARI: Which is like spitting straight up: It comes back to land on your own face.

ALISHAHI: Hence, your confession and claim are perfectly correct. The Rex Cinema was set on fire by you, in accordance with the SAVAK plan and the snitching of Mirsofyani, who is a fugitive now. Well, this is exactly what we are saying in this court.

HOSEYN: You are talking nonsense, Mr. Alishahi. In fact, the Rex Cinema wasn't supposed to be set on fire. We were supposed to set fire to any place we could, to create chaos in the city, so the people would come to the streets in demonstrations. Nobody told us to go and set the Rex Cinema on fire. Not even Mirsofyani said it. We said we needed gasoline. He said: Abdollah Lorqaba will get it for you. The rest was in our hands. First, we went to the office of the Rastakhiz Party, broke the windows, and threw in two Molotov cocktails.[43] This was two days before the Rex Cinema incident. But it didn't work. The Rastakhiz Party office had been closed for some time; nobody went there anymore; and even the furniture had been removed. Because the rooms were all empty, the fire did not catch on. As soon as smoke began to come out of the windows, people called the Fire Department and the fire was put out. Then we decided to find a cinema so that, first of all, it would be a place where the fire could not be put out quickly and there would be a few injured people, for publicity. We went to Soheyla Cinema. We bought tickets and went in. And we had our bags with us. We realized that we could be seen everywhere. There was a snack bar in the hallway, and everywhere you turned you could be seen. We left that place, too. We went to the Rex Cinema. We realized that that was the place for it. The auditorium was on the upper level, and the snack bar and ticket office were on the street level. In the middle of the movie we checked out the hallways and decided that that was the place. We left the theater and went to a teahouse nearby. We waited for the last show. We didn't even talk about it anymore. We were quite sure that this time our plan was going to work [*pause*], which it did.... [*Pause.*] Poor thing, Fallah. He went and bought three tickets. The movie had started. [*Pause.*] Farajollah started kidding around. He said, Don't forget the candles when you go to visit the shrine. He meant the pistachio nut bags. [*He is choked up.*]

ALISHAHI: What you've said still does not negate my theory.

JA'FARI: It only proves that you are guilty. You wanted a rope to hang yourself with. It is ready.

HOSEYN [*as if he is somewhere else*]: Those good guys. It isn't fair to talk about them like that.

[*ALISHAHI and JA'FARI leave the stage. Silence.*]

HOSEYN [*calmly and emotionally begins to murmur to himself*]: "Don't sit on the edge of our roof, / The rain will come and you'll get wet, / The snow will turn you to a ball, I bet, / And you'll roll into the painted pool."

[*Darkness.*]

Act III
Scene Three

This scene is performed in two separate forms, but simultaneously: 1) as a recorded videotape, from the TV monitors, and (2) live, on stage. In both, certain moments of action are timed to correspond with each other while others are unrelated.

On television monitors: the anthem of the Islamic Republic, accompanied by a popular revolutionary song. The voice of a MALE ANNOUNCER is heard during the ongoing anthem.

VOICE OF MALE ANNOUNCER: The Voice and Vision of the Islamic Republic reports from Abadan.

VIDEOTAPE OF FEMALE ANNOUNCER [*without make-up, in ill-fitting clothes and a scarf*]: In the name of the Almighty. Last night, the trial investigating the Rex Cinema tragedy, after fourteen open sessions which took place in the midst of the weeping and tears of the survivors of the victims of this tragedy, concluded its examination of the main perpetrators of the Rex Cinema fire, in which 389 innocent people lost their lives. Brother Alishahi, the prosecutor of the Rex Cinema revolutionary court trial, expressed his satisfaction with the results and said:

VIDEOTAPE OF ALISHAHI: It was very nice. The people really cooperated. I must especially thank the survivors of the victims, who were very understanding and most patient in the course of all the sessions of the trial, for encouraging us in the grave duty that was conferred on us. And I hope that with the support of the mobilized nation and the wise directives of the Leader of the Revolution, by holding even more revolutionary trials of this kind, we will be able to bring more of the enemies of the people and agents of the corruption of the regime of monarchical tyranny to the punishment they deserve for their actions. In any case, it was nice. It was very nice.

VIDEOTAPE OF FEMALE ANNOUNCER: Then Brother Hojjat al-Islam Ja'fari-Tabrizi, the presiding judge, announced the verdicts for the secondary and tertiary defendants as follows:

VIDEOTAPE OF JA'FARI: In the name of the Almighty. "There is such pleasure in forgiveness which is not found in revenge." In spite of the enemies of the revolution, who accuse the revolutionary courts of uncontrolled killings, in the Rex Cinema trial, with the exception of those persons who were directly involved in setting the fire, the defendants were sentenced to short-term imprisonment as follows: Colonel Khonafar, the man in charge of fire-fighting operations, who was not very successful in his work, two years; three police officers, two years; three workers in the cinema and five firemen, from one to three years.

VIDEOTAPE OF FEMALE ANNOUNCER: Concerning the implementation of the verdicts of the primary defendants, our reporter has prepared a taped report, which you will now see.

VIDEOTAPE OF MALE ANNOUNCER: At 2 am last night, the sentences of the primary defendants of the bloody, heart-rending Abadan Rex Cinema tragedy were implemented as follows: [*In a dim blue light on stage, the GOVERNMENT EMPLOYEE is seen being blindfolded.*] Farajollah Mojtahedi, SAVAK employee. He confessed to the court.

VIDEOTAPE OF EMPLOYEE:[44] We are bad. We are guilty. We are the enemy of the people, and we are whatever you say. . . .

EMPLOYEE [*on the stage*]: A glass of water. I am ill. My throat is dry. . . .

[*Shots fired on stage.*]

VIDEOTAPE OF EMPLOYEE [*reaction to being shot*]

VOICE OF MALE ANNOUNCER: The condemned man asked the people of Iran for forgiveness in his last moments.

[*On the stage two GUARDS bring the OWNER OF THE THEATER and blindfold him.*]

OWNER OF THE THEATER [*on stage*]: Where are you taking me? Leave me alone. [*Pause.*] What are you doing? I am innocent. I didn't do anything. . . .

VIDEOTAPE OF MALE ANNOUNCER: The next condemned man was the owner of the theater. He was a profiteering, money-hoarding individual who placed importance only on the huge income from the theater and basically paid no attention to the security and welfare of the clients of the theater. In the court he admitted his responsibility and guilt and said:

THE REX CINEMA TRIAL

VIDEOTAPE OF OWNER OF THE THEATER: I myself am a devotee of the revolution, a servant of the revolution. I am prepared to accept anything it dictates.

OWNER OF THE THEATER [*on stage*]: If you as much as touch a hair on my head, my family will avenge me. I am innocent. I didn't do anything.

[*Shots. Simultaneous action on stage and on television monitors.*]

VOICE OF MALE ANNOUNCER: Even in the last moments, he spoke of devotion to the revolution and asked the people to appreciate their own revolution.

[*On the stage, the OWNER OF THE THEATER is replaced with the MANAGER OF THE THEATER, and his eyes are blindfolded.*]

VIDEOTAPE OF MALE ANNOUNCER: The third convicted man was the manager of the theater, who was similar to the owner of the theater. His offense was announced in the court as mismanagement, misuse of his position, inattention and carelessness with regard to the safety of the theater, failure to employ experienced workers for services in the theater, and, on the whole, failure to feel responsible for the lives of his clients. He confessed:

VIDEOTAPE OF MANAGER OF THE THEATER: I don't intend to defend myself. [*Edited.*] I feel guilty.

MANAGER OF THE THEATER: My dear wife, take my children away from here. Tell them what kind of man I was. You, for one, know me. You know that I wouldn't hurt a fly. Goodbye, my dear wife.

[*Shots. Simultaneous action on stage and television. He is replaced with the COLONEL.*]

VIDEOTAPE OF MALE ANNOUNCER: At this time it was the turn of Colonel Amini. He was convicted of intentionally preparing a distorted report on the Rex Cinema and withholding the truth from the nation, in the interest of the regime, despite his expertise in anti-terrorism.

VIDEOTAPE OF COLONEL: No matter what judgment is made in this court about me, even if it is unjust and unfair, I consider it right and just.

COLONEL: "The friend who was raised to the top of the gallows / was only guilty of revealing the truth."[45] First they took away my freedom, then my homeland, then my religion, and then my life. The custom is that in the last moments, a man turns to God. But I, in these last moments, deny God. If God is the creator of devils like you, I deny God. I deny. . . .

[*Shot. Simultaneous action on stage and on television. The shot does not hit the COLONEL.*]

COLONEL [*on stage*]: Help! Help!

ALISHAHI: It missed him!

JA'FARI: Give it to me. [*Takes the GUARD's revolver and stands before the COLONEL.*]

COLONEL: Help!

[*Shot. Simultaneous action on stage and on television.*]

VOICE OF MALE ANNOUNCER: In the final moments, the COLONEL asked God to forgive him his sins.

[*On stage the COLONEL is replaced with LIEUTENANT BAHMANI.*]

VIDEOTAPE OF MALE ANNOUNCER: Of the police officers who were accused of cooperation or failure to prevent the Rex Cinema tragedy, three were sentenced to jail and one person condemned to death. First Lieutenant Manuchehr Bahmani was condemned to death.

VIDEOTAPE OF LIEUTENANT: I admit that what I did was wrong.

LIEUTENANT [*on stage*]: Don't blindfold me. I want to see the traitors of my country to the last moment. I don't want to forget their faces. Perhaps it is true that we will rise someday, and once again we will face one another. [*Shouts.*] Where are you, cleric? You said you would put the rope around my neck personally.

JA'FARI: Unfortunately, ropes are out of fashion. How about a bullet?

[*Approaches him with a revolver in hand.*]

LIEUTENANT: How about a spit? [*Spits towards him.*]

THE REX CINEMA TRIAL 177

[*Shot. Simultaneous action on stage and on television.*]

VOICE OF MALE ANNOUNCER: In his last moments Lieutenant Bahmani asked the president of the court to reduce his sentence. [*On stage LIEUTENANT BAHMANI is replaced with HOSEYN TAKBE'ALIZADEH.*] The last of the primary defendants was Hoseyn Takbe'alizadeh, who was convicted, along with two other people, of having received money from SAVAK to set the cinema on fire. At the trial, it was pointed out that these three had received the flammable materials and a can of poisonous gas from an Israeli agent.

VIDEOTAPE OF HOSEYN: I am telling you, I myself poured the gasoline on the doors. I myself struck the match of the Rex Cinema tragedy. Do I have to say it more clearly?

HOSEYN [*on stage, with nervous laughter in between his sentences*]: I tell this guard that my last wish as a condemned man is for him to sing "The Little Sparrow" with me. . . . He says . . ., he says . . . "Ask your mama to sing it!" I tell him . . . "My good man, my last wish is supposed to be granted, not yours . . . ha, ha. . . . No, all kidding aside. Don't turn me down, this last moment . . . sing with me . . . if you don't sing with me, I'll faint. Then, killing a person who has fainted will bring bad luck. . . ." Come on, sing. Heh, heh, heh. . . . "Who'll catch it . . . the sweeper man," heh, heh, heh. "Who'll kill it, his honor, the butcher man." Ha, ha, ha, ha!

[*Shot. Simultaneous action on stage and on television.*]

VOICE OF MALE ANNOUNCER: Takbe'alizadeh, who was weeping vehemently, said: "Ask the Imam of the People to mediate for me before God."

CLOSE-UP OF FEMALE ANNOUNCER: This concludes our report on the trial of the perpetrators of the Rex Cinema tragedy, which was presented to you by Brother Saber, the reporter of the Voice and Vision of the Islamic Republic. Now, with a final word from Hojjat al-Islam Ja'fari Tabrizi, we close the book on this heart-rending historical incident.

JA'FARI: "Hence, he who becomes an infidel is confused, and God shall not show the path to the oppressors."[46] "The main purpose is the image we leave behind / For I see that the world shall not last."[47] Upon the instructions of the Imam of the People, we wiped out one of the sinister and hated images of the cruel regime of monarchical tyranny. Of course, this would not have been possible but for the kind and magnificent generosity of our revered Christ-like leader. For, had it been otherwise, a person such as I would not have had the ability to face the difficulties and problems that, based on the tradition and history of the regime of monarchical tyranny, would have made adjudication and imposition of justice impossible. Of course, here I must express my gratitude to Brother Alishahi, the honorable prosecutor, who prepared the proof and evidence necessary against the defendants in the best possible manner and blocked the way for them to escape.

CLOSE-UP OF ALISHAHI [*nodding and smiling while fingering prayer beads*]: Wishing glory for the Moslem nation and health and a long life for our revered leader, the hope of the oppressed people of the world. May his blessing be lasting.

[*Close-up of JA'FARI changes into the insignia of the Islamic Republic, which fades with horror music. Darkness.*]

Act III
Scene Four

On the dark stage the DIRECTOR turns the hand-held spotlight on his own face, and then the light increases in the area where he is sitting, until his close-up appears on the television monitors through the camera, which is near him on a tripod. The DIRECTOR adjusts the microphone. Then he picks up a revolver off the tape player.

DIRECTOR: Jahan, my dear, I tape this part exclusively for you. [*He looks at his watch.*] It is now about 11 pm. I am holding a revolver and am sitting next to my camera on stage, which was where the Rex Cinema trial was held. [*Pause.*] Humph. Court of Justice. Justice. Judgment. No words in existence are more meaningless than those are for me. Perhaps they never existed. We, the simpletons, thought that they did. We went and sought them out, concerned ourselves about them and worked for them. [*Pause.*] Where are you, my Jahan, my love? Why weren't you with me? Why aren't you? Why, when we need each other more than ever, are we away from each other more than ever? Now, how can I explain to you what has happened to me all this time, what I have suffered? These bastards set fire to 389 living human beings while they were watching my movie. Then they forced me to tape and prepare a television report on the desecration of the blood of these very same people. Do you understand what this means? Even you, who are my shadow, my photographic negative, my heartbeat, they kept even you away from me. They kept you away from me under all sorts of pretexts, and I had to bear this huge, crushing steel cross alone on my shoulders. [*Pause.*] They promised me the position of deputy director of television. They tell me they will put me in charge of the second network. Bastards! They want to bribe me! I even tell you sincerely that I was tempted. Well, yes. When the final period to this conversation is going to be a bullet, why not at least confess to you? I thought about it. I said, "The second network!" Do you know what that means? That means the greatest opportunity to fight these bastards. That means the opportunity to communicate with millions of people and to turn the society upside down from the foundation. But now, at the end of this so-called trial, while I was packing up my junk, I asked myself: "Is it really necessary to turn the society upside down? Isn't revolution a kind of irreparable destruction? Has any revolution so far been reparable? This one shows that it is not. Is it possible to turn everything more upside down than this? And if it were, wouldn't it be again another deeper fall into the abyss of decadence?"

[*Pause.*] I don't know what shit history will make of this trial. My guess is it won't be able to find a more despicable, filthy trial than this in its memory. And it will never be able, in my opinion, to say enough about its heinousness. A few days ago, I read in the newspapers that because of the people's demand, the theaters damaged in the course of the revolution are supposed to be rebuilt with the help of the government. People's demand! The people have so soon forgotten the burned bodies of 389 of their compatriots and are once again rushing to the cinemas. They probably buy pistachio nuts from the shop next door to the theater and crack roasted melon seeds while watching the movie. [*Pause.*] To the mind of the society forgetfulness is, of course, an ordinary symptom. But what about us, whose profession is the cinema, who have loved the cinema, or at least made a living by it? How do we not feel a sense of responsibility towards the unjustly spilled and desecrated blood of so many human beings who were watching one of our works? The projectionist will return to his projection room. The ticket seller will sit in the box office. The cinema will operate. The cameraman will go behind the camera with his team once again. Actors will once again become each other's enemies, trying to snatch up their own stupid roles from each other. Again, trash after trash will be added to the garbage can of movies, and I, the so-called intellectual film maker, will again be tempted to mouth statements that would be pleasing in festivals so that, endorsed and financed by the same government that has come to power by burning human beings alive in the auditorium of a cinema, and to ensure its survival, has no qualms about burning hundreds of other movie theaters full of people, I will be able to take part in international film festivals. Shame on us! In this . . . in this sewer hole of the world, as Hedayat says,[48] we publish film magazines. We have a college for pictorial arts. We have critics who even write critical essays on the cinema of other countries. We do all . . . we . . . we, on each and every one of whose foreheads is branded forever the disgrace of the Rex Cinema, by our endorsement of this regime. I don't know what else to say. I don't . . . really . . . know . . . what to say.

[*Pause. He lifts the revolver and places the barrel to his temple.*]

If courage helps and I pull the trigger, promise me something: I don't want you to do anything for me. On the contrary, I want you not to do something. On my request or will, for the sake of love, friendship, husband and wife relationship, or anything else, as long as the government of the cinema burners is in power, don't ever go to a movie in this country. At least you, for one, don't go!

[*Darkness. Shot. Silence. The DIRECTOR's spotlight is turned on again. He is still alive.*]

It wasn't the sound of a shot. Don't be mistaken. It seems like a bulb or something exploded. I didn't say I would definitely pull the trigger. I said if courage helps me, which, of course, it did not. Come to think of it, this trigger can always be pulled. But the opportunity to become the president of the second television network does not always come up, to be Qotbzadeh's deputy.

[*Darkness. End.*]

The Rex Cinema Trial was first staged in March 1989 in Los Angeles, California, with the following cast:

Parviz Sayyad	MAS'UD TALA'I (the DIRECTOR)
Ali Pourtash	HOSEYN TAKBE'ALIZADEH
Houshang Touzi	ALISHAHI (the PROSECUTOR)
Ali Fakhr al-Din	JA'FARI-TABRIZI (the JUDGE)
Masha Manesh	LIEUTENANT BAHMANI
Shahram Brukhim	GOVERNMENT EMPLOYEE
Parviz Sayyad	OWNER OF THE THEATER
Kamran Nozad	COLONEL
Mohammad Ja'fari	MANAGER OF THE THEATER
Farideh Nazemi	TELEVISION ANNOUNCER
Farhad Barahman	TELEVISION ANNOUNCER

NOTES

1. On August 19, 1978, during the showing of "Gavazn-ha" (The Gazelles), a feature film directed by Mas'ud Kimia'i, at the Rex Cinema in Abadan, the theater was set on fire by arsonists apparently for political reasons. Although various groups were blamed by the government and the opposition for the fire, in which several hundred people lost their lives, and attempts were made prior to the Islamic revolution to identify the perpetrators, the case was not resolved even months after the revolution. Sayyad's play begins with preparations for the televised broadcast of the trial, which is to be directed and supervised by Mas'ud Tala'i (a lexical allusion to Kimia'i, since both *kimia* and *tala* mean gold in Persian); "Gavazn-ha" was considered to be a political statement against the Pahlavi regime.

2. "Gavazn-ha" is the story of two young Iranians, schoolmates who had gone their separate ways since they had seen each other some 10 years earlier. Seyyed, who was a popular athletic youth and was always the protector of his friend, Qodrat, has become a pathetic drug addict. Qodrat, on the other hand, has continued his education through college, but has become involved in anti-government political activities. While robbing a bank, Qodrat is wounded and has now come to stay with his old friend for a few days, eluding the police. Shocked by the transformation in his friend, Qodrat is able to awaken a sense of dignity in Seyyed. Ultimately, in a shoot-out with the police who have discovered Qodrat's hiding place, both friends die.

3. Hojjat al-Islam: a religious title for Shi'ite clerics.

4. "The Little Sparrow" song: a rendition of "Gonjishkakeh Ishi Mashi," a popular children's rhyme politicized through a symbolic rendition and sung by Farhad, a left-oriented popular singer. The theme song in the movie was sung by Pari Zangeneh, a well-known Iranian opera singer.

5. A city in northeast Iran and the site of the eighth Shi'ite Imam's Mausoleum, the holiest Shi'ite shrine in the country.

6. The Eighth Imam, Ali b. Musa al-Reza. The Refuge of Strangers is one of the many titles given him. The phrase "His Holiness did not want me" is a reference to the popular belief that you can go to Mashhad for pilgrimage only if the Eighth Imam permits you.

7. Ja'fari is a *seyyed* and hence believed to be a descendant of the Prophet Mohammad.

8. Minigroups [*goruhak-ha*]: a term used by the officials of the Islamic Republic to refer to dissident groups.

9. Amjadiyyeh: a sports stadium in Tehran where the Shah's birthday was celebrated every year on Aban 4 (26 October).

10. Ali Shari'ati (d. 1977): one of the chief ideologues of the Islamic Revolution in Iran. He opposed the Pahlavi monarchy and supported an Islamic form of government. Hoseyniyyeh Ershad was a religious center in Tehran where Shari'ati's followers gathered to listen to his speeches.

11. The Goethe Institute in Tehran sponsored poetry readings where large crowds gathered to hear poets give speeches or read their own poems. These gatherings were generally understood to be implicitly anti-government rallies. One such poetry evening occurred in 1977, which some consider to have been a triggering point of the 1978-79 revolution.

12. Ali Akbar: the son of the third Shi'ite Imam, who was martyred in Karbala in AD 680. The martyrs of the Karbala are in particular subjects for professional religious mourners, who sing about them at religious gatherings. The DIRECTOR's reference to JA'FARI's previous profession is implicitly pejorative.

13. Sadeq Qotbzadeh, a prominent figure in the early years of the revolution who was ultimately executed for plotting to overthrow the revolutionary government. At this time, Qotbzadeh was the director of Iranian television.

14. Network Two: a second television network that broadcast more sophisticated programming.

15. Fardin: Mohammad Ali Fardin, a movie actor particularly popular among the non-intellectual classes for portraying blue-collar characters.

16. Lines from a popular song in a nightclub scene from the movie "Qeysar." This was a critically acclaimed movie, directed by Mas'ud Kimia'i.

17. Shemr b. zel-Jowshan: the killer of Hoseyn, the grandson of the Prophet and the third Shiʿite Imam. See note 7 above.

18. Fereydun Farrokhzad: a singer of Western-style songs, generally disliked and ridiculed by traditional music enthusiasts. He hosted a television program that some considered a propaganda show for the Pahlavi regime.

19. In Persian, Sazman-e Ettela'at va Amniyyat-e Keshvar, generally referred to by its acronym, SAVAK.

20. *Khoms* and *zakat*: forms of religious tax incumbent upon a Moslem.

21. Thousand Families: reference to the richest families in Iran who received preferential treatment.

22. Tyrant: a rendition of *taghut*, a Koranic term used after the revolution to refer to the deposed shah and his regime.

23. Poem.

24. Koranic verse.

25. Poem.

26. The Fourteen Infallible Ones [*chahardah ma'sum*]: refers to the 12 Shiʿite Imams, the Prophet, and his daughter Fatimah.

27. Poem by Ferdowsi, the 10th-11th-century Iranian poet and author of the most important Iranian epic, the *Shahnameh* [Book of Kings].

28. Koranic verse.

29. Peykan: a small Iranian-assembled sedan version of the English car, the Hillman.

30. Leader of the Revolution: refers to Ayatollah Ruhollah Khomeini.

31. Aghasi: a popular singer and performer.

32. Zahhak: the mythological king on whose shoulders two serpents had grown. He had to kill young men and feed their brains to the two serpents.

33. See note 7.

34. The Sire of Martyrs [*Seyyed al-Shohada*]: reference to Hoseyn, the third Shiʿite Imam.

35. Qasem: the young nephew of Imam Hoseyn, who was also killed in the battle of Karbala. In this segment JA'FARI actually performs a religious mourning ritual [*rowzeh*] during which the listeners, overcome with emotion, weep for the martyrs of the battle of Karbala.

36. Kowsar Pond: believed to be in Paradise.

37. The corruptors of the earth [*mofsedin-e fi al-Arz*]: a phrase from the Koran that has been used by the Islamic government to refer to those who oppose it.

38. Farah is the name of Shah Mohammad Reza Pahlavi's wife. However, the former name of the mosque, Farahabad, may simply be coincidental.

39. During the 1978-79 revolution, Ayatollah Khomeini was quoted as saying that the shah must leave the country. Later, however, when the shah actually did leave and the revolutionaries took over power, they demanded his extradition to Iran from the various countries where he resided.

40. Arabic in the original.

41. "His Reverence" refers to Ayatollah Khomeini. Cassette tapes of his speeches were sold throughout the country in the months prior to the revolution.

42. Abujahl: literally "father of ignorance"; epithet the Prophet of Islam gave to Omar ebn al-Hesham, who opposed Islam.

43. The Rastakhiz ("Resurrection") Party was established in the 1970s by the shah as a means to rally support for his government and also to weed out the opposition, particularly from among the ranks of government employees. With the Rastakhiz, Iran in effect became a one-nation-one-party system. The nominal two-party system was thus succeeded by a monolithic political umbrella. Thus the headquarters of the Rastakhiz Party became the symbol of the shah's tyranny at its full command.

44. Video tapes recorded earlier by the DIRECTOR are edited by television authorities to suit what the officials wish to convey to the viewers.

45. This verse by Hafez (d. 1389) refers to Mansur Hallaj (858-922), the famous Sufi mystic, who was condemned to death for having said, "Ana al-haq" [I am the truth].

46. The Qur'an.

47. Poem.

48. Sadeq Hedayat (1903-1951), the best-known Iranian fiction writer in this century.